Mindset Matters in Trauma and Healing:

TRAUMA WORKBOOK

HOW TO MOVE FROM SURVIVING TO THRIVING DURING TRAUMA

Practical Biblical Principles for Overcoming Trauma & Triggers – Mentally and Somatically

ISBN: 979-8-9989216-0-5

Cover design by Rebecca A. Harris, Mindset Matters Publications.

First Edition: June 2025
Published by Mindset Matters Publications

Usage Notice

This workbook is intended for individual use or small group facilitation in accordance with the usage guidelines outlined herein. Individuals using this material for personal growth do not require licensing or formal training. However, churches, ministries, nonprofits, and other organizations seeking to use this content for mentoring programs, classroom instruction, or leadership training are required to complete authorized facilitator training and obtain written permission or appropriate licensing from Mindset Matters Communications, LLC. Unauthorized duplication, distribution, or reproduction of this material, in whole or in part, is strictly prohibited.

Permissions and Inquiries

If you have questions about usage rights, permissions, or bulk purchases, please contact Mindset Matters Publications at mindsetmatterspublications@gmail.com.

Licensing & Facilitation Notice

For inquiries about training, site licensing, additional resources, or keynote bookings, contact:
mindsetmatterscomm@gmail.com
www.mindsetmatterscommunications.com

HOW TO USE THIS WORKBOOK

This workbook is a flexible companion for renewing your mindset during trauma, or even years after. Whether you go through it alone, with a mentor, or in a group, each section strengthens your resilience and equips you to move from surviving to thriving — even before circumstances change. Your mindset matters deeply when facing the past, present, and future. Use this resource to align your thoughts with faith, hope, and God's truth.

Using Alone

- Move at your own pace — reflect on the Scriptures, journal, and apply the action steps.
- Pause when needed — healing is a journey, not a race.
- Use the prayer sections to seek God's wisdom and encouragement.

Using with a Mentor (Mentor Guide Available with Licensing)

- Share insights and challenges as you work through discussion questions.
- Invite accountability for applying new mindsets and spiritual habits.
- Allow room for prayer, encouragement, and wise counsel.

Using in a Group or Church Class (Mentor Guide Available with Licensing)

- Use sections as a guide for weekly meetings or group study.
- Read Scriptures, discuss reflection questions, and share journaling insights.
- Pray together for healing, resilience, and growth.
- Incorporate testimonies, activities, or teaching moments as needed.

Final Tip

This workbook is a flexible tool designed to support growth, not measure performance — letting God meet you wherever you are on the journey.

LEGAL DISCLAIMER

This workbook offers informational, educational, and spiritual enrichment content. It does not replace professional advice, counseling, diagnosis, or treatment. Always consult your physician, therapist, pastor, or another qualified health provider for any questions about your mental, emotional, physical, or spiritual well-being.

While this workbook provides immediate biblical encouragement, it does not substitute for clinical therapy or professional counseling. Use it as a supportive tool as you seek the Lord's guidance throughout your trauma and healing journey.

The Author and publisher do not accept responsibility for any adverse outcomes resulting from how you choose to apply the suggestions, techniques, or information in this workbook. You should consult appropriate professionals to address your personal needs and circumstances.

We have made every effort to present the concepts, techniques, and strategies included accurately. However, we do not guarantee specific results or outcomes.

By using this workbook, you agree to take full responsibility for your decisions, actions, and the results they bring.

Welcome to This Workbook!

I am so glad you have chosen to take this journey with me. My name is Rebecca, and like many of you, I have faced my share of trauma, heartache, and healing. Over the years, I have learned that it is not the challenges themselves but how we face them that shape our growth. At the core of this choice is our mindset. Mindset matters in trauma and healing — it shapes how we experience life's difficulties and determines our path to healing and growth.

This workbook serves as your companion on the journey toward healing, resilience, and personal transformation. It represents Phase One of **Thriving Life™** — a trauma and healing method — with each chapter offering interactive exercises, prayers, and reflections to help guide you toward a renewed sense of peace and purpose. The journey is not just about getting through difficult moments but learning how to thrive through them.

Whether going through a difficult time or seeking to grow in new ways, this workbook will offer practical tools and spiritual encouragement to keep moving forward. You are not alone in this journey. Together, we will explore how a transformed mindset can make all the difference in your healing process.

Let us walk this road together, with faith as our guide and God's promises as our foundation. You are stronger than you think — and through Jesus, you can overcome these challenges and thrive.

With gratitude and encouragement,

Rebecca Harris

Certified Trauma-Informed Coach | Christian Communicator | Author
Founder, Mindset Matters Communications, LLC.

TABLE OF CONTENTS

HOPE AND HEALING: A LETTER TO THE READER

If you are reading this, I want you to know that you are not alone in your pain, and my heart goes out to you. Whether you are working through this book alone or with a certified mentor, please understand there is hope even in the darkest times. Life can be tough, especially when you find yourself in moments of unbearable trauma. But as overwhelming as these moments may seem, you are not without guidance or support. This workbook aims to offer hope, serve as a tool for healing, and provide a roadmap to help you thrive — not just survive — through your most challenging circumstances.

I designed this workbook with you in mind because I have been where you are. I have faced trauma, seasons of darkness, and the overwhelming feeling of not knowing where to turn. Through years of personal experiences, faith, and healing, I have learned that we do not face trauma in vain. These challenging moments can be transformed into seasons of growth, peace, and renewal when we align our hearts with the truth of God's promises.

Jesus tells us that the number one thing we should do in life is to love God with all our hearts, souls, and minds (Matthew 22:37-38). But how do we do this when life seems to be falling apart? How do we love God in moments of deep pain or when we feel abandoned by everyone, including Him? The answer begins with understanding that we are not at war with flesh and blood but with spiritual forces (2 Corinthians 10:3). Trauma often has spiritual roots, and the Bible gives us clear guidance on how to fight and stand firm in the face of these trials (Ephesians 6:11-12).

The goal of this workbook is simple: to help you develop a deeper understanding of why your mindset matters and what role your body plays in the face of trauma. We will explore practical, biblical steps you can take to guard your heart and protect your peace. The Bible teaches us that the heart is central to our lives: "Guard your heart above all else, for it determines the course of your life" (Proverbs 4:23-27 NLT). Through the pages of this workbook, you will learn how to protect your heart, transform your mindset, and find peace even when the world around you feels like it is crashing down around you.

But more than that, this journey is not just about getting through the pain. It is about thriving in the midst of it. It is about moving beyond survival and stepping into a new chapter where your faith, resilience, and trust in God are stronger than ever. Jesus came so that we might have life and have it abundantly (John 10:10). This abundant life is possible even in trauma. This workbook will help guide you to it by laying out practical steps, easy-to-follow exercises, and Scriptures that you can apply to your daily life when the weight of your situation feels unbearable.

As you go through the steps in this workbook, I want to encourage you to embrace God's peace, which surpasses all understanding (Philippians 4:7). That peace is available to you no matter where you are in your healing process. I pray that as you lean into His Word, you will find the strength to walk in faith, step by step, and discover your resilience. As you walk this path, I pray that you will come to understand the words of Paul: "I have learned to be content whatever the circumstances... I can do all this through Him who gives me strength" (Philippians 4:11-13). You, too, can find that contentment, that peace, and that strength — not in your power but through Jesus, who strengthens you.

CHAPTER ONE
Things to Know to Get Started

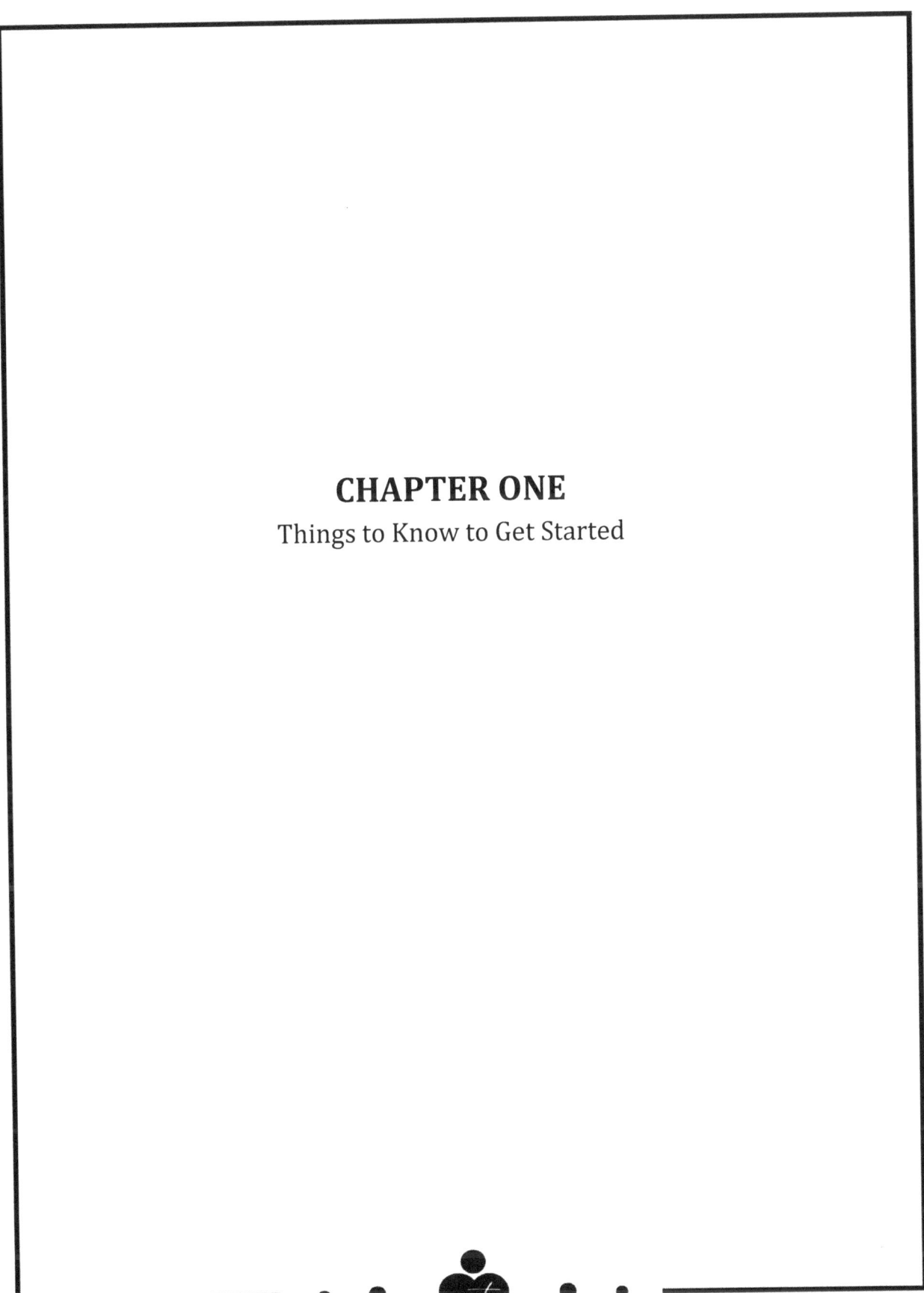

THINGS TO KNOW TO GET STARTED

WHAT THE BIBLE SAYS ABOUT TRAUMA

While the Bible does not define trauma directly, it speaks to the realities of deep suffering and the human experience of hardship. God desires to heal, comfort, and restore those who are hurting. Scripture teaches that Jesus' followers are not abandoned and offers hope for the hurting through faith in Jesus.

WHY MINDSET MATTERS

The Bible repeatedly reminds us of the importance of guarding our thoughts and hearts. Romans 12:2 calls us to "Be transformed by the renewing of your mind." This transformation is key to walking in victory and healing, especially when trauma seeks to cloud our hearts and minds. How we think shapes how we heal, which is why **mindset matters in trauma and healing**.

When we change how we think and focus on God's truths, we allow Him to renew our minds and give us the strength to endure. Philippians 4:8 encourages us to focus on what is true, noble, and praiseworthy. As we move through the exercises in this workbook, we will learn how to make this shift — to focus on God's promises rather than our pain and embrace the truth that healing is possible even in the most challenging circumstances.

Mindset is not just a concept — it is how we navigate spiritual warfare. 2 Corinthians 10:3-5 teaches us that our battle is not against flesh and blood but against spiritual forces. Through this workbook, we will learn Biblical principles and how to use them to fight spiritual warfare, identify and resist the enemy's lies, and renew our minds through God's Word.

This **SHIFT** of mindset during trauma is critical because what happens in our minds directly affects our hearts. As Proverbs tells us, our hearts determine the course of our lives (Proverbs 4:23). When we choose to let God transform our minds, we are not just making it through this season — we are positioning ourselves to thrive and walk in God's abundant life.

WHAT ROLE THE BODY PLAYS

The Bible clearly distinguishes between the soul and the body (1 Thessalonians 5:23). The soul — mind, will, and emotion — represents a person's inner, eternal aspect. In contrast, the body refers to the physical aspect. Although these are distinct, they are closely connected, especially in the process of healing from trauma. Somatic awareness helps us recognize and acknowledge the body's signals during stress or trauma, providing insight into how our physical state relates to our emotional and spiritual well-being.

When we learn how to connect to our "Felt Sense" — the body's experience or signals — during the moments of trauma and triggers, we can enter into the complete **REST** found only in Jesus. This concept of the "Felt Sense" is foundational in somatic trauma work and was introduced by Eugene Gendlin and later developed in the field by Peter Levine (Levine, 1997). We can experience healing and peace for both soul and body through understanding our body's responses in these moments. Although we may feel physically burdened by life's struggles, Jesus promises His burden is light, and we will find rest for our souls (Matthew 11:28-29).

This workbook gives us practical steps to apply biblical truths in our daily lives, helping us move beyond survival and live victoriously. We remember that healing is a journey. We take it one step at a time, trusting that God walks with us through every moment.

DEFINING TRAUMA

Before diving into the practical steps that help us move from surviving to thriving, let us first look at what trauma is — and what it is not. There are many ways to define trauma, so we will begin with a general definition and then briefly explore specific contexts to help us recognize what we are experiencing. Based on my training as a Certified Trauma-Informed Coach and personal experience, I offer the following explanation as a helpful framework for processing trauma.

 What Trauma Is:

Trauma is an emotional response to a life-altering or deeply distressing event. It occurs when an event's impact overwhelms a person's ability to cope, often leaving them feeling helpless, unsafe, or unable to regain a sense of normalcy. Trauma exists on a spectrum, meaning its effects can vary in severity depending on the individual and the circumstances. If left unresolved, trauma can lead to self-destructive behaviors, such as self-medicating, and may contribute to the development of personality disorders.

 What Trauma Is Not:

If you have been in the church for any length of time, you have likely heard terms like hardship, storm, crisis, chaos, testing, trial, struggle, suffering, tribulation, and affliction. These are a few words that describe life-altering events that challenge us deeply. While these events leave us fundamentally changed, they are not trauma — at least not in the way we are defining it. **Trauma is not an event.**

Life-altering events fall into several categories:

1. Relational – Conflicts, betrayals, breakups, divorce, or losing a loved one.
2. Physical Health – Severe illness, injury, disability, or domestic/sexual abuse
3. Mental Health – Depression, anxiety, emotional abuse, or breakdowns.
4. Financial – Bankruptcy, unemployment, debt, or sudden financial loss.
5. Career/Professional – Job loss, career transition, workplace conflict, or business failure.
6. Spiritual/Existential – Crises of faith, loss of purpose, or major spiritual awakenings.
7. Social – Bullying, public humiliation, or exclusion from social groups.
8. Environmental/Natural – Natural disasters like earthquakes, floods, or hurricanes.
9. Cultural/Identity – Discrimination, identity crises, or struggles with belonging to a community.
10. Legal – Involvement in lawsuits, criminal accusations, or imprisonment.

 *The Different Variations of Trauma:*

Let us look at trauma in specific contexts to help you recognize what you might be experiencing. The following trauma categories are an educational summary adapted from principles found in trauma psychology, somatic therapy, and developmental research (see Other Sources of Material, page 127).

1. Emotional or Psychological Trauma
This type of trauma occurs when an overwhelming experience disrupts a person's emotional well-being or sense of safety. It often leads to feelings of fear, anxiety, and avoidance of reminders of the event.

2. Physical Trauma
Physical trauma refers to injuries caused by external forces, such as accidents or violence. While it directly affects the body, it can also lead to emotional trauma.

3. Acute Trauma
Acute trauma results from a sudden and intense event, such as a natural disaster, accident, or assault. This type of trauma often triggers strong emotional reactions, including shock and fear.

4. Chronic Trauma
Chronic trauma develops from ongoing exposure to harmful situations, like prolonged abuse or neglect. It results in a long-lasting emotional response that impacts a person's well-being over time.

5. Complex Trauma
Complex trauma occurs when a person experiences repeated, distressing events, particularly within close relationships, such as in cases of childhood abuse or domestic violence. It can profoundly affect emotional stability and relationships.

6. Secondary Trauma
Secondary trauma arises when someone experiences emotional distress by witnessing or hearing about another person's traumatic experiences. This form of trauma is common in caregivers, first responders, or anyone in a supportive role.

7. Developmental Trauma
Developmental trauma happens during childhood when a child faces repeated negative experiences, like manipulation, neglect, or abuse. These early experiences can disrupt emotional and psychological development and lead to long-term effects, including difficulties with emotional regulation, self-esteem, attachment, and coping mechanisms.

8. Historical or Generational Trauma
This type of trauma affects a group of people who share a collective experience, such as systemic oppression or genocide. The emotional impact often passes down through generations.

9. Somatic Trauma
Somatic trauma occurs when unresolved emotional pain manifests physically. It can lead to chronic tension, pain, or other physical symptoms, reflecting the body's response to emotional distress.

Take a moment to reflect on your current situation. Highlight or circle the words that resonate with what you are experiencing right now. Journal your thoughts on the lines below. See Appendix A for multiple charts to help you process (pages 109-112).

Journal:

_____

_____

_____

_____

_____

_____

_____

_____

_____

_____

_____

_____

_____

_____

_____

_____

_____

_____

_____

_____

_____

_____

WHAT IS HAPPENING IN OUR MIND DURING TRAUMA

Understanding the terms and categories of life-altering events and trauma can bring clarity and help us process what we are going through. As we move through the workbook, remember that the practical steps presented are not specific to any event or variation of trauma. They apply to various situations regardless of age, gender, income, education, family structure, race, ethnicity, or life circumstances.

Events do not hold meaning or emotion — we assign meaning to them. When something traumatic happens, the nervous system kicks into survival mode. If the nervous system remains unregulated — unable to return to a balanced state — the body can stay stuck in patterns of hyperarousal or hypoarousal, better known as fight, flight, freeze, or fawn (Appendix A, page 113). This occurs when the amygdala, the part of our brain that processes emotions and forms memories, senses danger and reacts by attaching negative emotions like fear or anxiety to the event (van der Kolk, 2014).

The amygdala essentially "hijacks" the experience, causing our body to react as though there is imminent danger. In this workbook, when we refer to the amygdala "hijacking" the experience, we are using the term metaphorically to describe how the amygdala takes over the body's responses, making the nervous system react as if the threat is still present, even after the actual danger has passed.

These reactions, however, are not always connected to the present moment. Past trauma — especially experiences from childhood — can shape how we respond to situations today. Emotional memories often settle deep in our subconscious. When something in the present reminds us of a past hurt, our amygdala can trigger a reaction that feels as intense as the original event. In those moments, we might instinctively respond as if the old threat is happening all over again, even when the current situation does not truly call for it. Over time, these subconscious patterns shape how we think, feel, and behave — often without realizing it.

While we could explore the science further, for this workbook, it is enough to know that our minds and bodies respond to past and present trauma. The techniques in these pages will help us catch this "hijacking" early so we can interrupt automatic responses before they take over. As we grow aware of how the amygdala and past experiences shape our reactions, we begin to regain control over initial reactions and take intentional steps toward healing. This awareness is part of the mindset shift that moves us from surviving trauma to truly thriving — in new challenges and when old wounds resurface.

The spiritual disciplines introduced here — such as prayer, gratitude, and worship — are designed to nurture holistic Christian growth. They foster the transformation of the heart, soul, and mind, leading to tangible outward expressions of faith, such as worship and self-control. Just as trauma exists on a spectrum, so does healing. These practical steps will help some more than others, and seeking clinical counseling is always wise for extra support during the healing journey.

THIS WORKBOOK

As we progress through the upcoming chapters, we will learn two frameworks that can guide our mindset transformation and bring our body to rest, empowering us not just to survive but to thrive when facing trauma and triggers. No matter where we start, the journey ahead will draw us closer to God, help us discover our resilience, and equip us with the strength to move forward with hope.

"You can't go back and change the beginning, but you can start where you are and change the ending."

- C.S. Lewis

CHAPTER TWO
The Greatest Commandment and Our Mindset –
SHIFT Framework

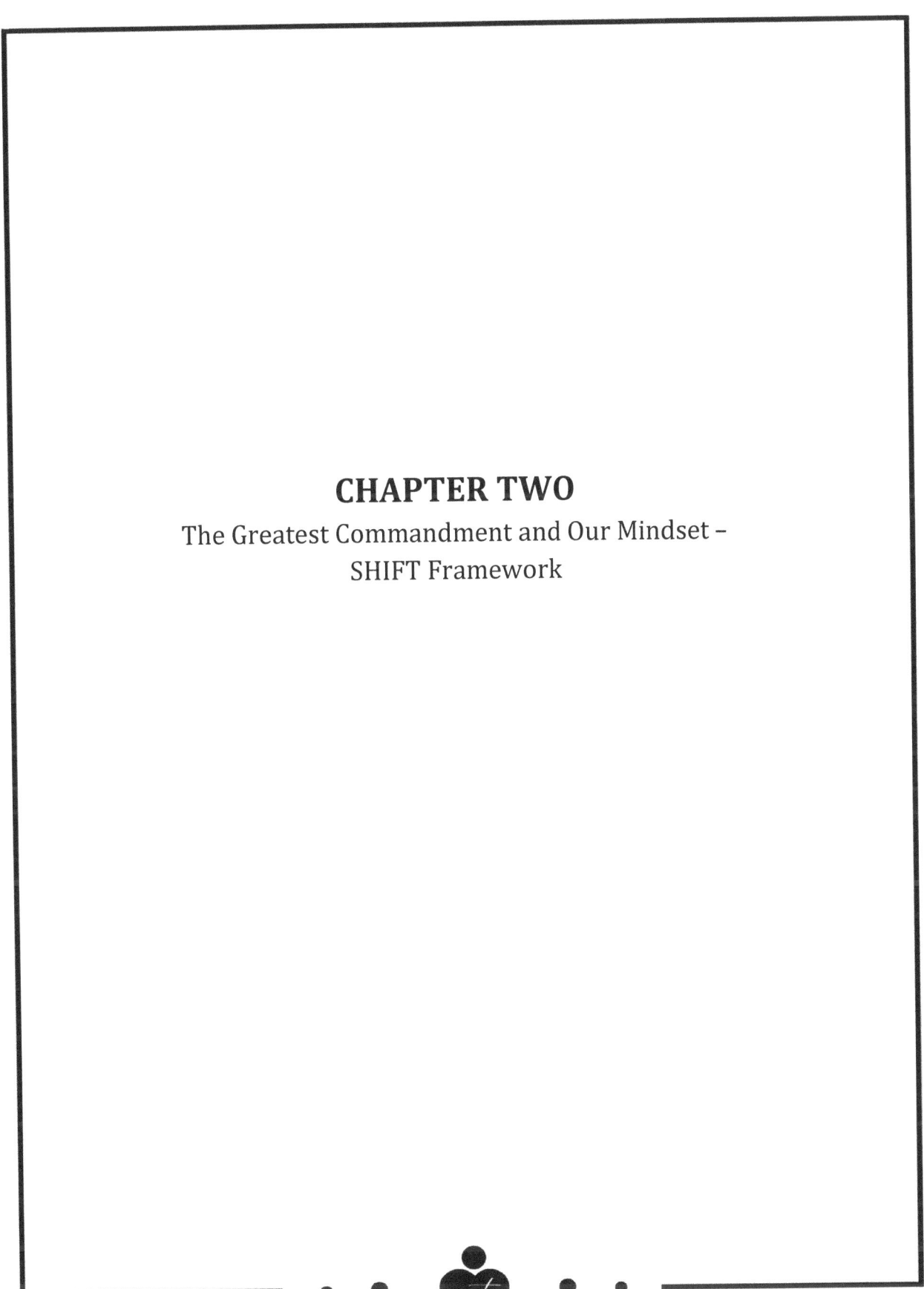

THE GREATEST COMMANDMENT AND OUR MINDSET

SHIFT FRAMEWORK

The Bible consists of many commandments — the greatest is to love the Lord with all your heart, soul, and mind (Matthew 22:37-38). Heart, soul, and mind represent our core aspects — our will, emotions, intellect, and identity. This workbook will consider these interconnected aspects as a unified concept — **MINDSET**.

To follow the greatest commandment, we must cultivate the right mindset — one focused on loving God fully with all our being. This mindset is essential, especially amid trauma, as it helps guide our responses and actions in alignment with God's Truth. Trauma can cloud our thinking, but a mindset rooted in God's Word empowers us to respond with faith, hope, and love, even under challenging circumstances.

When we intentionally shift our mindset toward God, we allow Him to transform our hearts and minds, leading us to more profound healing and a closer relationship. As we engage with these exercises, we will learn practical ways to strengthen our mindset, ensuring that it aligns with God's greatest commandment to love Him fully, no matter the events and circumstances we face.

Numerous Scriptures emphasize the importance of mindset. Write out the following passages and underline what stands out to you:

Proverbs 4:23-27 (NLT): _____

_____

_____

_____

_____

Romans 8:6-8: _____

_____

_____

_____

_____

2 Corinthians 10:3-5: _____

_____

_____

_____

Psalm 139:23-24: _____

_____

_____

_____

_____

Colossians 3:1-2: _____

_____

_____

_____

_____

Philippians 2:5: _____

_____

_____

_____

_____

Reflect on what you have learned about the importance of your mindset from these Scriptures. Which verses stood out to you most and why?

_____

_____

_____

_____

What did you find encouraging and hopeful from dwelling on these passages?

_____

_____

_____

_____

_____

_____

_____

_____

_____

_____

_____

_____

_____

_____

_____

PRACTICAL STEPS WITH THE SHIFT FRAMEWORK

To cultivate a healthy mindset during overwhelming trauma, when even daily tasks seem impossible, we must not only learn the practical steps outlined in the following chapters but also commit to remembering and applying them. Shifting our mindset, despite the circumstances, is not a one-time task — rather, it is a deliberate process of retraining our thoughts and habits. This daily practice reshapes the subconscious, enabling us to thrive through and beyond life-altering events.

These steps are organized into the acronym **SHIFT** to make learning and applying the principles more manageable during trauma.

SHIFT

To move from surviving to thriving during trauma, we must undergo a shift in our mindset. The **SHIFT** framework teaches us how to transform our natural reactions and align our perspective with God's truth, focusing on "the things above" (Colossians 3:2). This shift plays a key role in the speed and quality of our healing. **SHIFT** is one of two frameworks in this workbook that we can use to help manage and even prevent the "hijacking" of our nervous system, creating the opportunity for healing during trauma — even if circumstances have not changed yet.

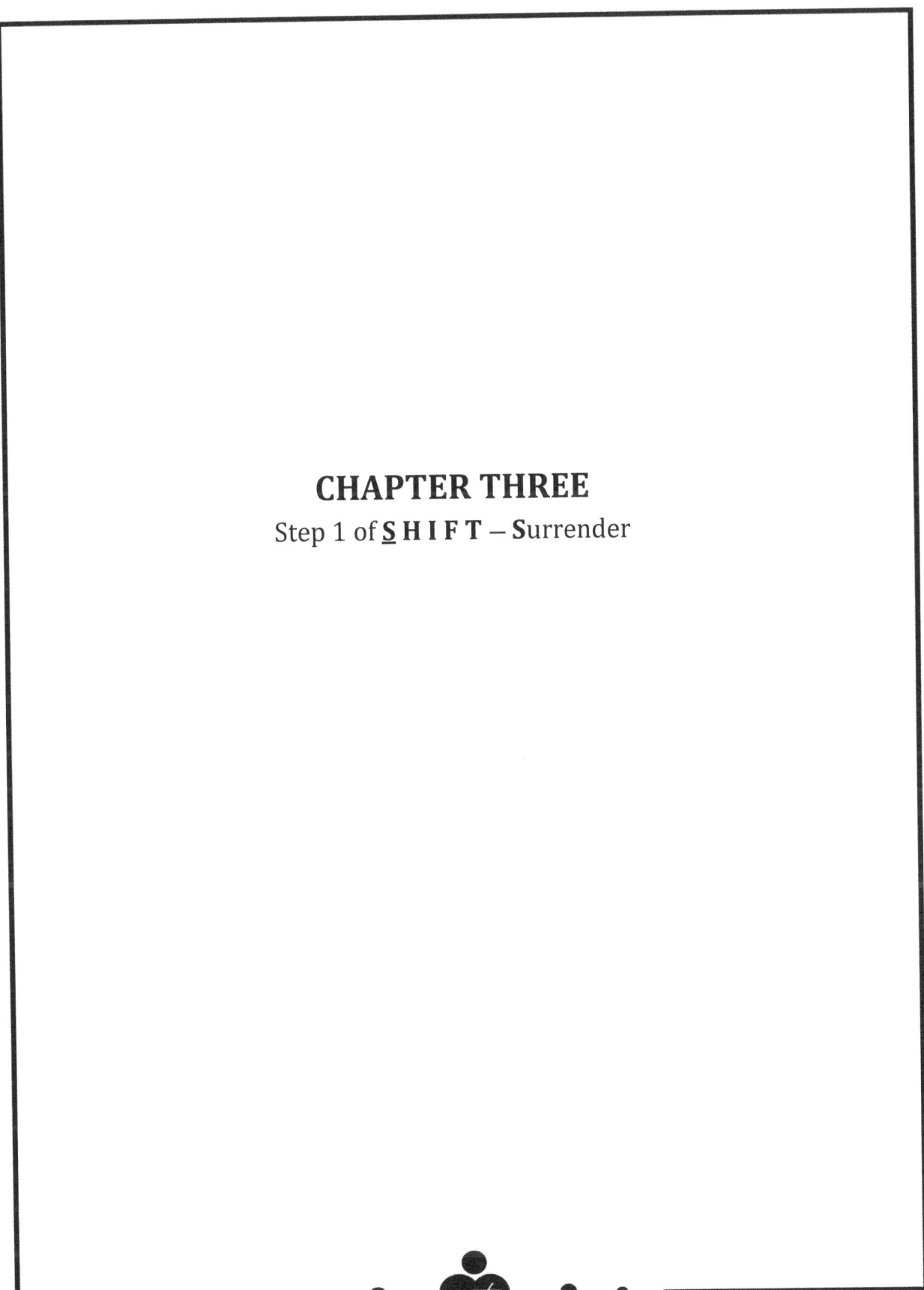

CHAPTER THREE
Step 1 of **S** H I F T — Surrender

STEP 1 OF **SHIFT** – SURRENDER

Action: Surrender to God's Plan   **How:** Pray   **Result:** Faith & Obedience

A PATH TO CHOOSE

"Enter by the narrow gate. For the gate is wide and the way is easy that leads to destruction, and those who enter by it are many. For the gate is narrow and the way is hard that leads to life, and those who find it are few." – Matthew 7:13-14

When standing in the face of trauma, you are immediately met with a choice — a first step. The path you choose will determine your healing journey. One path is wider, looks more appealing, and some argue it is easier. The other path is narrower, more challenging to navigate, and intimidating to approach.

The first option is the one of the flesh — the path of least resistance. You have the most control when going down this road, or so you believe. The focus is on fulfilling your desires and choosing whatever makes you feel good. It leads to self-medication, whether that is through drugs, alcohol, sex, binge-watching shows, and so on.

The second choice is the path of surrender — surrendering your will to God's will. As you progress along this road, you have to give up complete control of your circumstances and come to terms with not having all the answers. The focus is drawing near to Jesus, walking in obedience to His Word, and trusting fully in what you cannot see, which leads to hope and rejoicing despite the circumstances.

WHAT PATH WILL YOU CHOOSE

When faced with trauma, our choices can shape our healing journey. Take this short assessment to explore which path you are inclined to take or want to take. Answer honestly and reflect on your responses.

Assessment: Which Path Will You Take in the Face of Trauma?

1. When you are overwhelmed by trauma, your first instinct is to:

A) Distract myself with something that makes me feel better in the moment.
B) Pray, journal, or seek guidance through God's Word.

2. How do you typically handle feelings of uncertainty?

A) I take control and make decisions based on what feels easiest or most comforting.
B) I acknowledge my lack of control and ask God for direction, even if it feels hard.

3. What will you most likely do when facing pain or emotional distress?

A) Turn to habits like binge-watching shows, eating, drinking, or other activities to numb the pain.
B) Seek support from prayer, worship, or a trusted spiritual mentor.

4. Which of the following best describes your mindset in adversity?

A) "I need to focus on myself and get through this, however I can."
B) "I need to trust in God's plan, even if I do not understand it yet."

5. How do you feel about surrendering control of your situation?

A) It is uncomfortable; I feel safer when I am in control.
B) It is freeing, even though it requires faith and patience.

Results:

☐ Mostly A's: You may currently lean toward the path of the flesh, seeking control and immediate relief. While this path may seem easier initially, it can lead to more struggles over time. Consider how relying on God's strength and surrendering your will could offer more profound, lasting healing.

☐ Mostly B's: You are inclined toward the path of surrender, choosing to trust God and walk in obedience despite the difficulty. This path requires faith and perseverance but leads to hope, peace, and spiritual growth.

☐ A Mix of A's and B's: You might be standing at the crossroads, torn between comfort and surrender. Reflect on what truly brings healing and how trusting God could transform your journey.

Take a moment to reflect on your results. What path are you looking down? What first step can you take right now to choose a different path?

Journal:

_____

_____

_____

_____

_____

_____

_____

_____

_____

WHAT IS SURRENDER

Surrendering to God's plan, or will, is the acknowledgment — through word and deed — that you are allowing God to take control of the past, present, and future. You are telling Him with your words that you know He knows all and knows best. You are showing Him with your actions that you are willing to deny your desires by obeying Him. **Surrendering means entirely relying on God's strength to overcome your challenges.**

Read the following Scripture and fill in the blanks:

Matthew 16:24-26
"Then Jesus told his disciples, 'If anyone would come after me, let him deny himself and take up his cross and follow me. For whoever would save his life will lose it, but whoever loses his life for my sake will find it. For what will it profit a man if he gains the whole world and forfeits his soul? Or what shall a man give in return for his soul?'"

1. I must deny my desires and _____ Jesus' lead.

2. Whoever would _____ his life will lose it, but whoever loses his life for God's sake will

_____ it.

What stands out to you from the above passage? _____

_____

_____

_____

HOW DO I SURRENDER

"Watch and pray that you may not enter into temptation. The spirit indeed is willing, but the flesh is weak." — Matthew 26:41

This first step of the **SHIFT** framework is so crucial, and when you are truly ready to release control and trust God's will for your life, it is pretty simple. Start talking to God — **pray.** Talk to Him, yell at Him, mumble, or quietly lie flat on your face. Praying without ceasing is one part of God's will for you (1 Thessalonians 5:17-18).

Once you start talking to God, you will learn how He speaks to you. As you connect with God and release control, the Holy Spirit will guide you in your prayers. Praying is not about eloquence or knowing the "right words," but relying on the Spirit to help you communicate with God.

Read the following Scriptures and fill in the blanks:

Romans 8:26-27
"Likewise the Spirit helps us in our weakness. For we do not know what to pray for as we ought, but the Spirit himself intercedes for us with groanings too deep for words. And he who searches the hearts knows what is in the mind of the Spirit, because the Spirit intercedes for the saints according to the will of God."

1. The Spirit helps me in my _____, for when I don't know how to pray, the Holy Spirit

_____ for me with _____ too deep for words.

2. God knows every heart's innermost thoughts, desires, and motives. Because the Holy Spirit

_____ for me, even when I don't know how to pray or what to ask for, the Spirit ensures my

prayers are consistent with God's _____/purpose.

Matthew 26:36-39
"Then Jesus went with them to a place called Gethsemane, and he said to his disciples, 'Sit here, while I go over there and pray.' And taking with him Peter and the two sons of Zebedee, he began to be sorrowful and troubled. Then he said to them, 'My soul is very sorrowful, even to death; remain here, and watch with me.' And going a little farther he fell on his face and prayed, saying, 'My Father, if it be possible, let this cup pass from me; nevertheless, not as I will, but as you will.'"

1. When Jesus' soul was very _____, to the point that He felt as if He were dying, Jesus

went off by himself and _____.

2. Jesus fell on his _____ and prayed, saying, "My Father, if it be possible, let this cup pass from

me; nevertheless, not as I will, but as you _____."

Look up and read the following Scriptures and write down what stands out to you:

Matthew 14:23: _____

_____

Mark 1:35: _____

_____

Mark 6:46: _____

_____

Luke 5:16: _____

_____

Luke 6:12: _____

_____

Luke 9:18: _____

_____

What did Jesus do in each of these passages?

He went off by _____ and _____.

As you persevere in your trauma through prayer, you begin cultivating a life of steadfast prayer. This type of prayer is not just an isolated event. Instead, it is a continuous, faithful communication with God and a reflection of your reliance on God as you begin to experience the depth of God's work in your life. Steadfast prayer invites you to surrender your plans and trust God in every situation.

THE RESULT OF SURRENDERING

As you entirely rely on God's strength to overcome your challenges, a distinct calmness will begin to set into your soul. Offering your life and circumstances as a living sacrifice leads to transformation and the ability to discern God's will. This leads to a level of faith in your Lord and Savior, which gives birth to a desire and hunger to learn and the strength to obey His Word. **Surrendering to God's plan will result in faith and obedience.**

Read the following Scriptures and fill in the blanks:

Jeremiah 29:11-14
"For I know the plans I have for you, declares the LORD, plans for welfare and not for evil, to give you a future and a hope. Then you will call upon me and come and pray to me, and I will hear you. You will seek me and find me, when you seek me with all your heart. I will be found by you, declares the LORD, and I will restore your fortunes and gather you from all the nations and all the places where I have driven you, declares the LORD, and I will bring you back to the place from which I sent you into exile."

1. The Lord promised the Israelites that when they _____ upon Him and pray to Him, He would

_____ them.

2. When I seek the Lord with all of my _____, I will _____ Him.

Romans 8:28-29
"And we know that for those who love God all things work together for good, for those who are called according to his purpose. For those whom he foreknew he also predestined to be conformed to the image of his Son."

1. God's will works all things together for _____, for those who have a relationship with Him through faith in Jesus and are _____ according to His purpose.

2. The call refers to His initiative in the salvation of drawing people to Himself for His glory, and for the believers to be _____ to the image of His _____.

John 14:15
"If you love me, you will keep my commandments."

1. If I love God, I will keep His _____.

2. If I _____ God, obedience will be the natural outflow, resulting in complete surrender of myself – my past, present, future, shame, hurts, dreams, and plans.

James 1:22
"But be doers of the word, and not hearers only, deceiving yourselves."

1. True obedience is not just _____ God's Word but acting upon it, which reflects genuine surrender to His will.

2. When I am a hearer of the Word only, I _____ myself.

Hebrews 11:1-3
"Now faith is the assurance of things hoped for, the conviction of things not seen. For by it the people of old received their commendation. By faith we understand that the universe was created by the word of God, so that what is seen was not made out of things that are visible."

1. Faith means I have the _____ of what I hope for and the _____ of what I do not see.

2. By faith, I understand that the _____ was created by the _____ of God.

When you believe God's will works all things together for good, and embrace his sovereignty, you begin to surrender to His purpose for your life. **Faith is believing God is who He says He is and that He will do what He promises.** As you surrender to God, you begin to live out this faith. Letting go of control, seeking God through prayer, being obedient to His will, and embracing this faith marks the beginning of true healing, shifting you from merely surviving through trauma to beginning to thrive.

PERSONAL APPLICATION

Remember, this journey is not about perfection but perseverance. Through perseverance, you build resilience, growing stronger with each challenge. Keep praying, as prayer strengthens your connection with God. Keep believing and trusting His good plan, even in uncertainty. Keep surrendering, letting God lead you through each trigger. Know that God is with you every step, supporting you, helping you grow and heal, and shaping you more like Jesus.

Additional Scripture for Reflection:

Hebrews 5:7-10
"In the days of his flesh, Jesus offered up prayers and supplications, with loud cries and tears, to him who was able to save him from death, and he was heard because of his reverence. Although he was a son, he learned obedience through what he suffered. And being made perfect, he became the source of eternal salvation to all who obey him, being designated by God a high priest after the order of Melchizedek."

1. What areas do you need to surrender more fully to the Holy Spirit in prayer?

_____

_____

_____

_____

2. What steps can you take today to move closer to healing through surrender?

_____

_____

_____

_____

Journal:

_____

_____

_____

_____

_____

A NEW BEGINNING: ACCEPTING JESUS AND WALKING IN FAITH

"Let those who fear the Lord say, 'His steadfast love endures forever.' Out of my distress I called on the Lord; the Lord answered me and set me free." - Psalm 118:4-5

If you have journeyed through this workbook and realized that you do not have a personal relationship with Jesus, know it is never too late to begin. True healing and transformation start with Him. No matter your past, His love is unconditional, His grace is abundant, and He desires a relationship with you.

Salvation is a gift from God that you receive by placing your faith in Jesus. If you are ready to surrender your life to Him and step into a new beginning, pray this prayer from your heart:

Prayer of Salvation:

"Heavenly Father, I come before you, acknowledging that I need you. I confess that I am a sinner in need of your grace. I believe that Jesus died for my sins and rose again so that I may have eternal life. Today, I choose to turn away from my old ways and surrender my life to you. Jesus, be my Lord and Savior. Please fill me with your Holy Spirit, guide me in truth, and help me to walk in your will. Thank you for your love, your forgiveness, and the new life I have in you. In Jesus' name, Amen."

If you prayed this prayer, welcome to the family of God! Your journey with Jesus begins now, and He walks with you every step of the way.

Next Steps in Your Faith Journey

 Plug Into a Bible-Based Church – Surround yourself with other believers who can encourage and strengthen you in your walk with God. A local church is where you can grow in your faith, learn more about God's Word, and find support in your healing journey.

 Get Baptized – Baptism is a public declaration of your faith in Jesus. It represents being buried with Him in His death and raised into a new life with Him (Romans 6:4). If you have accepted Jesus, take the next step and be baptized as a testimony of your faith.

 Seek God Daily – Build a personal relationship with God through prayer, worship, and studying the Bible. Let Him lead you as you continue to heal, grow, and walk in His purpose for your life.

God has an incredible plan for you, and this is just the beginning of a new life filled with His love, grace, and restoration. Keep pressing forward, knowing that He is with you, guiding you every step of the way.

ADDITITIONAL RESOURCES

Memory Verses:
- "Pray without ceasing." (1 Thessalonians 5:17)
- "Count it all joy, my brothers, when you meet trials of various kinds, for you know that the testing of your faith produces steadfastness. And let steadfastness have its full effect, that you may be perfect and complete, lacking in nothing." (James 1:2-4)
- "And he said to all, 'If anyone would come after me, let him deny himself and take up his cross daily and follow me. For whoever would save his life will lose it, but whoever loses his life for my sake will save it.'" (Luke 9:23-24)
- "Cast your burden on the Lord, and he will sustain you; he will never permit the righteous to be moved." (Psalm 55:22)
- "Submit yourselves therefore to God. Resist the devil, and he will flee from you. Draw near to God, and he will draw near to you. Cleanse your hands, you sinners, and purify your hearts, you double-minded." (James 4:7–8)
- "Do not be anxious about anything, but in everything by prayer and supplication with thanksgiving let your requests be made known to God." (Philippians 4:6)
- "Love your enemies and pray for those who persecute you." (Matthew 5:44)
- "Though I walk in the midst of trouble, you preserve my life; you stretch out your hand against the wrath of my enemies, and your right hand delivers me." (Psalm 138:7)
- "Finally, be strong in the Lord and in the strength of his might." (Ephesians 6:10)
- "I have been crucified with Christ. It is no longer I who live, but Christ who lives in me. And the life I now live in the flesh I live by faith in the Son of God, who loved me and gave himself for me." (Galatians 2:20)
- "May all who seek you rejoice and be glad in you! May those who love your salvation say evermore, 'God is great!'" (Psalm 70:4)
- "For this is the love of God, that we keep him commandments. And his commandments are not burdensome. For everyone who has been born of God overcomes the world. And this is the victory that has overcome the world – our faith. Who is it that overcomes the world except the one who belives that Jesus is the Son of God?" (1 John 5:3-5)

Quick Prayers:
- "Lord, have mercy on me."
- "Father, give me strength to keep moving."
- "Lord, let your presence calm my heart and guide me toward healing."
- "Father, I surrender my desires to you and believe you are working all things for my good."
- "Lord, I give my pain to you. Heal my heart, transform my life, and lead me into a future full of hope."

Closing Prayer:
"Lord, teach me to live a life of steadfast prayer. Help me surrender to your Spirit, release my pain, and trust you in all things. Fill my heart with faith, hope, and trust as I seek your presence through every circumstance. In Jesus' name, Amen."

Things to Try:
- Journal your prayers.
- Pray out loud.
- Kneel beside your bed when praying.
- Lie flat on your face in quietness and listen.

CHAPTER FOUR

Step 2 of **S <u>H</u> I F T** – Hear

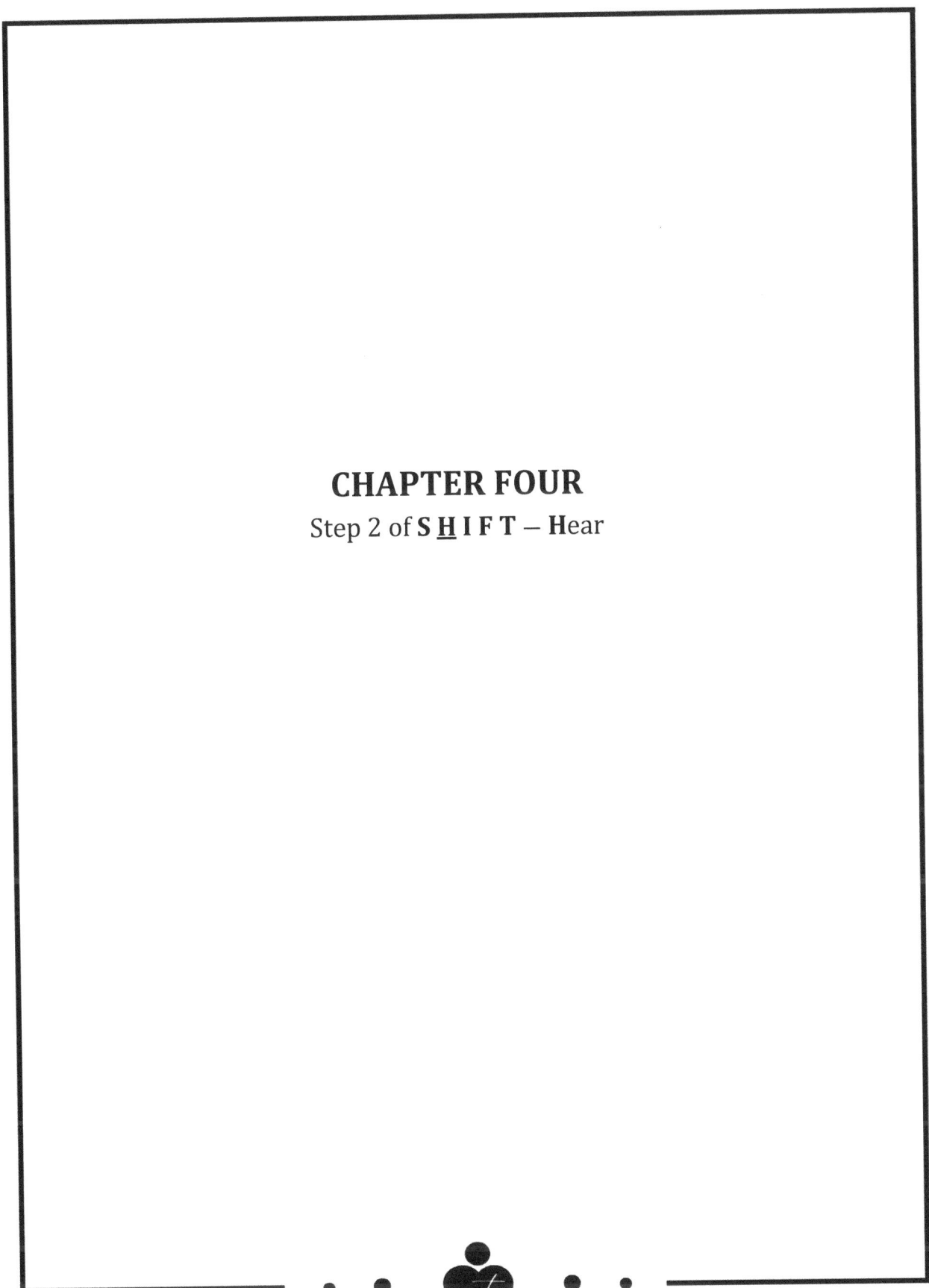

STEP 2 OF **SHIFT** – HEAR

Action: Hear God's Voice   **How:** Be in the Word   **Result:** Humility & Thanksgiving

A PATH CHOSEN

At this point in your journey, you have made a choice. You are either walking down the path of the flesh or surrendering to God's plan. When you relinquish control over your circumstances, you can move forward confidently, even when the future remains uncertain. As you learned in the previous chapter, the first step to shifting your mindset during trauma is surrendering to God's will for your life by seeking Him in prayer, leading to faith and obedience in Jesus.

Understanding God's will starts with learning to recognize His voice in your daily life. How do you know what His will is? How do you ensure your decisions align with His guidance? What changes when you truly hear God's voice?

This next step is the second most crucial part of the **SHIFT** framework — right after surrendering your control to God's will. As you understand and apply what it means to hear His voice, you open the door to deep healing, even in the middle of trauma.

WHAT DOES IT MEAN TO HEAR

"So faith comes from hearing, and hearing through the word of Christ." – Romans 10:17

Trauma feels overwhelmingly lonely, scary, confusing, heartbreaking, exhausting, and painful. In these moments, you often find yourself sifting through a flood of thoughts, information, and advice, trying to make sense of it on your own.

So what do you do? You listen for God's voice. Hearing God means tuning in to His words above all others. His voice gives you the clarity and direction to make decisions that align with His will, no matter what circumstances surround you.

Hearing God's voice means recognizing His guidance, which brings clarity and direction in any circumstance. His guidance helps you feel steady, even when everything else feels uncertain. His voice brings comfort to your soul and wisdom to your choices. In the middle of trauma, His voice becomes the anchor that grounds you and the light that leads you toward healing.

Read the following Scriptures:

Isaiah 30:21
"And your ears shall hear a word behind you, saying, 'This is the way, walk in it,' when you turn to the right or when you turn to the left."

John 10:27
"My sheep hear my voice, and I know them, and they follow me."

What stands out to you from the above passages? _____

_____

_____

HOW DO I HEAR

"Your word is a lamp to my feet and a light to my path." – *Psalm 119:105*

Hearing God's voice is about discerning His will for your life and following His direction amid the countless thoughts and advice that flood your mind. **Hearing is only possible through being in the Word.** By understanding how God speaks, you can take every thought captive, follow His lead, and find the strength to move forward. This process starts by reading and studying God's Word.

With so many voices competing for your attention, you must test every thought against God's truth. As you seek His confirmation, He removes distractions, reveals His path, and brings clarity even in uncertainty. The more you listen and obey, the more you recognize His voice in every step of your journey. The following three steps will guide you as you learn to recognize and respond to His voice:

❶ *Be in the Word of God Ahead of Time:*

The Word should be part of your daily life through apps, reading plans, or devotionals. Staying immersed in Scripture helps you handle challenges, discern God's voice, and grow in faith — not only personally, but also through the support of church and community. Meditating on God's Word day and night allows you to trust His truth over your understanding. He promises to make your ways prosperous and be with you wherever you go (Joshua 1:8–9).

Read the following Scriptures and fill in the blanks:

John 8:31–32
"So Jesus said to the Jews who had believed him, 'If you abide in my word, you are truly my disciples, and you will know the truth, and the truth will set you free.'"

As I abide in the Word, I grow as a disciple of Jesus. I know the _____, and the _____

sets me _____.

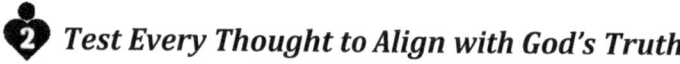 *Test Every Thought to Align with God's Truth:*

God calls you to test every thought to ensure it aligns with God's truth, discerning whether it comes from God, yourself, others, or the enemy (Deuteronomy 11:16). Staying in the Word equips you to recognize God's voice and separate it from deceptive, accusatory, or selfish thoughts. Romans 12:1-2 calls you to refuse conformity to this world and embrace transformation by renewing your mind to discern God's will clearly.

Voice Distinctions:

- **God's Voice:** Brings peace, truth, and guidance aligned with Scripture (John 10:27, Isaiah 30:21, Philippians 4:7)
- **The Enemy's Voice:** Deceptive, accusatory, and promotes sin (John 8:44 NIV, Revelation 12:10, Genesis 3:1-5)
- **The Flesh:** Seeks selfish pleasure and immediate gratification (Galatians 5:17, Romans 8:6-7, James 1:14-15)
- **Peers:** Influenced by societal norms, sometimes misaligned with God's will (Romans 12:2, Proverbs 13:20, 1 Corinthians 15:33)

Understanding these distinctions helps you discern the spiritual origin of thoughts and influences you encounter daily (for a more in-depth look, see Appendix B). To understand the enemy and his tactics more deeply, see Appendix C.

Read the following Scripture and answer the questions.

1 John 4:1–2
"Beloved, do not believe every spirit, but test the spirits to see whether they are from God, for many false prophets have gone out into the world. By this you know the Spirit of God: every spirit that confesses that Jesus Christ has come in the flesh is from God."

I do not believe every _____, but I _____ each one to see whether they are from God. I know

a spirit is of God if it _____ that Jesus is the Christ and has come in the flesh.

1 Thessalonians 5:16-22
"Rejoice always, pray without ceasing, give thanks in all circumstances; for this is the will of God in Christ Jesus for you. Do not quench the Spirit. Do not despise prophecies, but test everything; hold fast what is good. Abstain from every form of evil."

I do the will of God by _____ always, _____ without ceasing, and giving _____ in

all circumstances. After testing every thought, I hold fast to what is _____, just as He commands me.

Look up Deuteronomy 11:18-19.

How does Moses expresses the importance of being in God's word daily: _____

_____

_____

_____

_____

❤3 *Speak Scripture to the Lies:*

Your mind is a spiritual battlefield. In hard times, fear, anxiety, and doubt can creep in, and the enemy tries to flood your thoughts with lies. But God gives you His Word as a weapon. When you speak and stand on Scripture, you push back darkness and anchor your thoughts in truth.

Remember that God is omnipresent and omnipotent, while the enemy is neither. God is everywhere, fully aware of your heart before you even think. The enemy is limited. Satan cannot be everywhere at once, so he sends his demons to carry out his work. He cannot read your mind but listens to your words and uses life's common struggles to lead you astray.

Read the following Scripture and fill in the blanks:

2 Corinthians 10:4-5
"For the weapons of our warfare are not of the flesh but have divine power to destroy strongholds. We destroy arguments and every lofty opinion raised against the knowledge of God, and take every thought captive to obey Christ."

1. My weapons for warfare are not of the _____, but of the Spirit, and it allows me to destroy those lies brought against God when I take every thought captive.

2. I destroy arguments and lies by taking every thought _____ to obey _____.

Explore these possible lies that come up in the face of trauma. Practice speaking the Scriptures to the lies you relate to with the included Scripture Affirmations:

Affirming Truths:

- Lie: "I am not good enough."
  Truth: "My grace is sufficient for you." (2 Corinthians 12:9)

- Lie: "God has forgotten me."
  Truth: "He will never leave you nor forsake you." (Deuteronomy 31:6)

- Lie: "I will always be stuck."
  Truth: "God works for the good of those who love him." (Romans 8:28 NIV)

- Lie: "I cannot overcome this temptation."
  Truth: "He will provide a way out." (1 Corinthians 10:13 NIV)

- Lie: "My mistakes define me."
  Truth: "I am doing a new thing." (Isaiah 43:18-19)

- Lie: "I am unworthy of God's love."
  Truth: "While we were still sinners, Christ died for us." (Romans 5:8)

What specific lie has the enemy been trying to make you believe recently?

_____

_____

_____

Which Scripture from above, or from your own quite time, speaks directly to that lie? Write it down and repeat it out loud whenever the lie tries to creep in.

_____

_____

How has speaking God's truth brought clarity or strength into your current circumstances?

_____

_____

What additional Scriptures can you find to speak against other common lies the enemy uses in your life?

_____

_____

As you begin reading your Bible, journal what God is opening your eyes to about your trauma. What is He revealing about your past, present, and future?

_____

_____

_____

_____

_____

_____

_____

THE RESULT OF HEARING

"I will instruct you and teach you in the way you should go; I will counsel you with my eye upon you."
- Psalm 32:8

God is ready to guide and counsel you through His voice, offering direction and wisdom. As you seek His voice, you will begin to see more clearly — whether regarding your past, present, future, or all of the above. His truth will free you, lifting the weight of loneliness, pain, and fear while cultivating gratitude for the journey.

Hearing God's voice will result in humility and thanksgiving, as you recognize your need for His wisdom over your understanding. From this posture of humility, forgiveness and repentance naturally follow — freeing your heart from bitterness and aligning you with His mercy. In this freedom, gratitude takes root as you see His faithful hand leading you through every trial with love and purpose.

Read the following Scriptures and fill in the blanks:

Forgiveness:

Ephesians 4:32
"Be kind to one another, tenderhearted, forgiving one another, as God in Christ forgave you."

Because God in Christ forgave me, I choose to extend _____ and compassion to others.

Luke 6:36
"Be merciful, even as your Father is merciful."

As I hear God's voice and understand His _____, I actively extend that same compassion to others.

 **Repentance:**

Acts 3:19
"Repent therefore, and turn again, that your sins may be blotted out."

When I _____, I turn away from sin and receive forgiveness and restoration from God.

2 Peter 3:9
"The Lord is not slow to fulfill his promise as some count slowness, but is patient toward you, not wishing that any should perish, but that all should reach repentance."

God patiently waits for me to come to _____, inviting me to return to Him and live.

Thanksgiving:

1 Thessalonians 5:18
"Give thanks in all circumstances; for this is the will of God in Christ Jesus for you."

God calls me to give _____ in _____ circumstances.

Colossians 3:15-17
"And let the peace of Christ rule in your hearts, to which indeed you were called in one body. And be thankful. Let the word of Christ dwell in you richly, teaching and admonishing one another in all wisdom, singing psalms and hymns and spiritual songs, with thankfulness in your hearts to God."

As I let the _____ of Jesus dwell in me, thanksgiving will naturally flow from my heart.

Hearing God's voice and understanding His mercy allows you to see your circumstances more clearly without taking them personally. This change in perspective helps you forgive others, recognizing that God's grace covers both you and them. Repentance, acknowledging your sin and turning back to God, brings freedom and renewal. Your relationship with God deepens with humility and gratitude, allowing you to see His goodness even in trauma. Embracing His mercy helps you appreciate His presence and faithfulness in all circumstances.

As your faith grows and you continue to hear God's voice, you experience a shift in your mind and decisions, leading to greater freedom and choices that reflect your healing and transformation.

PERSONAL APPLICATION

You face countless thoughts every day, but to thrive in trauma, you must focus on your mindset. Capturing every thought is not a one-time task — it is a daily practice that becomes foundational as you move from surviving to thriving. Proverbs 4:23 reminds you to guard your mind, for it determines the course of your life. What you choose to FOCUS on will either lead to life or destruction — you must dwell on what is right.

Refer to the FOCUS framework in the Healing Workbook for additional guidance during the healing process after trauma.

Read the following Scripture:

Philippians 4:6-8

"Do not be anxious about anything, but in everything by prayer and supplication with thanksgiving let your requests be made known to God. And the peace of God, which surpasses all understanding, will guard your hearts and your minds in Christ Jesus. Finally, brothers, whatever is true, whatever is honorable, whatever is just, whatever is pure, whatever is lovely, whatever is commendable, if there is any excellence, if there is anything worthy of praise, think about these things."

What stands out to you from the above passage? _____

_____

_____

_____

_____

List 8 things found in the above passage that you should be dwelling on:

1. _____   5. _____
2. _____   6. _____
3. _____   7. _____
4. _____   8. _____

To respond to life's challenges with obedience rather than emotion, you must stay anchored in God's Word, test everything that comes your way, and actively speak Scripture over the lies that seek to deceive you.

As you move into the next step of the **SHIFT** framework — Invite In — remember that through continuous communion with God, you remain anchored and receive the strength to stand firm in your faith. Persistent prayer and the discipline of capturing every thought are not separate practices but are deeply connected as you grow spiritually.

"Whatever keeps me from the Bible is my enemy, however harmless it may appear to be."
— A.W. Tozer

ADDITIONAL RESOURCES

Memory Verses:

- "We destroy arguments and every lofty opinion raised against the knowledge of God, and take every thought captive to obey Christ." (2 Corinthians 10:5)
- "Bearing with one another and, if one has a complaint against another, forgiving each other; as the Lord has forgiven you, so you also must forgive." (Colossians 3:13)
- "Oh give thanks to the Lord, for he is good, for his steadfast love endures forever!" (Psalm 107:1)
- "Your word is a lamp to my feet and a light to my path." (Psalm 119:105)
- "Jesus answered them, "Truly, truly, I say to you, everyone who practices sin is a slave to sin. The slave does not remain in the house forever; the son remains forever. So if the Son sets you free, you will be free indeed." (John 8:34-36)
- "For you were called to freedom, brothers. Only do not use your freedom as an opportunity for the flesh, but through love serve one another. For the whole law is fulfilled in one word: 'You shall love your neighbor as yourself.'" (Galatians 5:13-14)
- "You make known to me the path of life; in your presence there is fullness of joy; at your right hand are pleasures forevermore." (Psalm 16:11)
- "Out of my distress I called on the Lord; the Lord answered me and set me free." (Psalm 118:5)

Quick Prayers:

- "Lord, teach me how to hear your voice."
- "Father, give me strength to do your will."
- "Lord, open my eyes to your truth."
- "Father, I surrender my anger to you. Help me to forgive those who have done me harm."
- "Lord, help me to capture every thought as I seek to do your will."

Closing Prayer:

"Lord, give me wisdom and understanding to recognize your voice. Show me what areas of my life I need to surrender to you. Open my eyes to anyone I need to forgive, and give me the strength to follow your will. Thank you for guiding, strengthening, and loving me through this difficult time. In Jesus' name, Amen."

Things to Try:

- Listen to the Bible through a Bible App.
- Get a creative journaling Bible if you like coloring while listening or reading.
- Journal your dreams — God may be speaking to you through your subconscious.
- Start a praise song list for songs that stand out to you during the trauma.
- Engage in a regular bible study.

Appendix B:
Quick Guide — Four Voices

Appendix C:
Going Deeper — Learning the Enemy

CHAPTER FIVE
Step 3 of **S H I F T** — Invite In

STEP 3 OF **SHIFT** – INVITE IN
Action: Invite in God's Grace **How:** Through Gratitude **Result:** Self-Control & Peace

GOD'S GRACE

You have now come to a crucial crossroads. To have made it this far, you must have already chosen the path of surrendering to God's plan — relinquishing control over your circumstances and moving forward, even when the future remains uncertain. You have done this through prayer, seeking and hearing God's voice, capturing every thought, and testing everything against His truth in the Word. Step one has led to faith and obedience, while step two has brought you to a place of humility and thanksgiving. Now, you face another decision. Will you continue to practice these steps daily with fervor, or will you falter and fall back onto the path of the flesh — taking control and seeking relief in ways that only numb the pain?

Like all aspects of spiritual growth, the results of the previous steps are not a one-time victory. You must choose daily to live in humility and thankfulness despite the trauma you are facing. If you do not, bitterness and resentment can sneak in like a virus, leading you down a destructive path. By now, you may feel utterly exhausted — overwhelmed by new revelations, counseling, and the weight of spiritual warfare. But I urge you to stand firm because it is in this very place that God's grace will powerfully meet you after taking this next step. After this step, His grace will take over and carry you through the remaining steps of the **SHIFT** framework.

The third step in the **SHIFT** framework is to invite God's grace into your heart through gratitude. God's grace sustains you when you cannot go on. It empowers you to continue to be thankful in the midst of pain and to keep pressing forward even when you are weary. His grace will lead you through the trauma and into healing, transforming you along the way.

WHAT DOES IT MEAN TO INVITE IN GOD'S GRACE

Inviting God's grace begins with humbly acknowledging the need for Him in every area of life. It means receiving His undeserved favor with a heart full of gratitude. Grace cannot be earned — God freely offers it through Jesus Christ as an expression of His kindness and power. His grace forms the foundation of salvation and provides ongoing strength through every trial, temptation, and season of growth.

Living in God's grace means embracing His forgiveness and depending on His strength — rather than relying on personal effort. Let His truth shape thoughts, guide actions, and renew attitudes. Grace saves (Ephesians 2:8-9), and grace continues to grow a life rooted in holiness, hope, and healing.

A heart that invites in grace is also a heart that cultivates gratitude. Gratitude flows naturally from recognizing God's love, mercy, and presence as undeserved gifts. As 1 Thessalonians 5:18 says:

"Give thanks in all circumstances; for this is the will of God in Christ Jesus for you."

A grace-filled life adopts thankfulness as its posture. It recognizes blessings, even when they come through hardship. And it walks daily in dependence on the Holy Spirit — with confidence in God's faithfulness, not personal ability.

HOW DO I INVITE IN GOD'S GRACE

"Do not be anxious about anything, but in everything by prayer and supplication with thanksgiving let your requests be made known to God." — Philippians 4:6

You invite God's grace into your life by cultivating a posture of prayerful gratitude. While grace is a gift you cannot earn, your openness to receive it often begins with a heart that turns to God with thankfulness — not just in moments of blessing, but especially in times of need.

Living in thanksgiving is an intentional daily choice. It means looking beyond circumstances and acknowledging God's presence and provision, even when things are hard. As you bring your concerns, hopes, and needs to Him in prayer — with thanksgiving — you create space for His peace, strength, and guidance to enter in.

Receive God's grace not through striving, but by inviting Him into every situation with a thankful and humble heart — **having an attitude of gratitude.** Explore these ways to invite in:

Read the following and fill in the blanks.

 Gratitude: Acknowledging God's Goodness (Grateful Heart)

God invites you to focus on His goodness in moments of anxiety, worry, or confusion. As you choose gratitude, you shift your attention from what you lack to the blessings surrounding you.

James 1:17 reminds you:

"Every good gift and every perfect gift is from above, coming down from the Father of lights, with whom there is no variation or shadow due to change."

Recognizing that all good things come from God fills you with thanksgiving. This mindset helps you see life through the lens of God's provision, not scarcity.

1. "Every good and perfect gift comes from _____."

2. "I will give thanks to God for _____, even when I feel _____."

Additional Scripture for Reflection:

"Oh give thanks to the Lord, for he is good; for his steadfast love endures forever!" (Psalm 107:1)

"Let us come into his presence with thanksgiving; let us make a joyful noise to him with songs of praise!" (Psalm 95:2)

What daily blessings have I overlooked that I need to thank God for?

_____

_____

_____

_____

_____

_____

_____

_____

_____

_____

_____

_____

2 *Humility: Recognizing God's Sovereignty (Grateful Submission)*

The final component of thanksgiving is humility — acknowledging that everything you have comes from God. Humility positions your heart to receive His grace with grateful submission, understanding that you can do nothing without God.

John 15:5 is a good reminder of this powerful truth:

"I am the vine; you are the branches. Whoever abides in me and I in him, he it is that bears much fruit, for apart from me you can do nothing."

Humility allows you to live in a posture of dependence on God. It reminds you that your abilities, resources, and even your breath are His gifts. As you acknowledge God's sovereignty, you also recognize your need for His guidance and provision, leading you to live with a spirit of thanksgiving.

Psalm 100:4 invites you into this attitude of gratitude:

"Enter his gates with thanksgiving, and his courts with praise! Give thanks to him; bless his name!"

When you humbly come before God, recognizing His greatness and your dependence, you can't help but respond with thanksgiving.

Fill in the blanks:

1. "I will humbly acknowledge that without God, I am _____, but with Him, I can _____."

2. "I will live in gratitude by submitting to God's _____ and trusting in His _____."

Additional Scriptures for Reflection:

"Humble yourselves, therefore, under the mighty hand of God so that at the proper time he may exalt you." (1 Peter 5:6)

"For from him and through him and to him are all things. To him be glory forever. Amen." (Romans 11:36)

In what areas can I practice more humility, recognizing that all I have comes from God?

_____

_____

_____

_____

_____

_____

_____

_____

_____

_____

_____

_____

_____

_____

_____

THE RESULT OF INVITING IN GOD'S GRACE

"And let the peace of Christ rule in your hearts, to which indeed you were called in one body. And be thankful." – Colossians 3:15

Inviting in God's grace will result in self-control and peace. A grateful heart anchors your emotions and thoughts in God's truth, especially in seasons of trauma or uncertainty. His grace brings clarity in confusion, strength in weakness, and peace in chaos — not because circumstances are perfect but because His presence is real.

Living in thanksgiving becomes more than a practice — it becomes a way of life. As you acknowledge God's goodness, embrace His timing, and submit to His sovereignty, your heart begins to rest in His peace. This peace guards your mind, strengthens your faith, and shapes your perspective so that thankfulness becomes your natural response — no matter the circumstances.

Read the following Scriptures and fill in the blanks:

2 Timothy 1:7
"For God gave us a spirit not of fear but of power and love and self-control."

God does not give me a spirit of _____, but of _____ and _____.

Romans 8:6
"For to set the mind on the flesh is death, but to set the mind on the Spirit is life and peace."

God calls me to take action and set my _____ on the Spirit.

When I set my mind on the _____ I will experience life and _____.

What do you see God's grace working in your life right now?

_____

_____

_____

_____

_____

_____

_____

_____

_____

PERSONAL APPLICATION

"My grace is sufficient for you, for my power is made perfect in weakness." – 2 Corinthians 12:9

By surrendering your will to God, you exercise faith and embrace a life of obedience. This act of yielding to Him allows His wisdom and guidance to shape your life, leading you closer to His perfect purpose. When you choose to listen to God's voice, you also open yourself to His gifts of humility — repentance and forgiveness — and thanksgiving. His voice speaks peace into your heart, reminding you of His love and the abundant grace He freely gives.

As you invite His grace into your life with an attitude of gratitude, His peace and self-control empower you. Gratitude strengthens a heart that stays steadfast and grounded, equipping you to respond with patience, humility, and calm — even in life-altering circumstances. In each moment, choose to receive God's sustaining presence, embrace His steady peace, and walk in His strengthening grace.

Be mindful of your thoughts and stay in His presence as you move forward in your trauma. Healing has already started — He will sustain you.

Read the following Scriptures and fill in the blanks:

Colossians 2:6–7
"Therefore, as you received Christ Jesus the Lord, so walk in him, rooted and built up in him and established in the faith, just as you were taught, abounding in thanksgiving."

Being rooted in Jesus, having faith that He is who He says He is and will do what He promises, I will

naturally abound in _____.

2 Peter 1:5–7 NIV
"For this very reason, make every effort to add to your faith goodness; and to goodness, knowledge; and to knowledge, self-control; and to self-control, perseverance; and to perseverance, godliness; and to godliness, mutual affection; and to mutual affection, love."

After I am rooted in faith, I am to move forward with action by adding goodness, knowledge,

_____, brotherly affection, and love in my daily life.

Proverbs 4:23
"Keep your heart with all vigilance, for from it flow the springs of life."

This verse emphasizes the importance of guarding your thoughts and emotions because what you focus on shapes who you are. As you align your heart and mind with God's love and stay in His presence, He calls you to show others the same love and compassion. To do this, you must practice self-control. Self-control is a fruit of the Spirit, given by God, and enables you to live in a way that honors Him.

- If I want to live in forgiveness, I cannot dwell on the past.
- If I want to be in God's presence, I can't harbor hatred.
- If I want peace, I must let go of resentment.
- If I want to reflect God's love, I must show compassion, even when it is difficult.
- If I want to grow spiritually, I must take every thought captive and align it with God's truth.
- If I want to experience joy, I must cultivate a heart of gratitude.
- If I want to walk in freedom, I must resist the urge to control or manipulate situations.
- If I want to live out God's plan, I must choose humility over pride.

What areas of your life do you need to accept with gratitude, trusting that God has a greater plan?

_____

_____

_____

_____

What specific areas would you like to be more self-controlled in?

_____

_____

_____

_____

How has God's grace brought healing or strength into your current circumstances?

_____

_____

_____

_____

What additional Scriptures can you find to speak on self-control in your life?

_____

_____

_____

_____

_____

_____

_____

_____

_____

_____

_____

_____

_____

_____

_____

_____

_____

_____

_____

Remember, God loves you deeply, and His grace is sufficient to carry you through every challenge and trauma. His presence is always with you, offering comfort, hope, and healing.

Jeremiah 29:11

"For I know the plans I have for you, declares the Lord, plans for welfare and not for evil, to give you a future and a hope."

Although originally spoken to the Israelites, this promise reflects God's unchanging character. It affirms that His plan leads to restoration, peace, and hope regardless of circumstances. Trust Him. Walk in surrender. As you lean into His will, you will experience the steady peace of knowing He walks with you every step of the way.

ADDITIONAL RESOURCES

Memory Verses:

- "Let us then with confidence draw near to the throne of grace, that we may receive mercy and find grace to help in time of need." (Hebrews 4:16)
- "Give thanks in all circumstances; for this is the will of God in Christ Jesus for you." (1 Thessalonians 5:18)
- "Every good gift and every perfect gift is from above." (James 1:17)
- "Humble yourselves, therefore, under the mighty hand of God so that at the proper time he may exalt you." (1 Peter 5:6)
- "Keep your life free from love of money, and be content with what you have, for he has said, 'I will never leave you nor forsake you.' So we can confidently say, 'The Lord is my helper; I will not fear; what can man do to me?'" (Hebrews 13:4-6)
- "Praise the Lord! I will give thanks to the Lord with my whole heart, in the company of the upright, in the congregation." (Psalm 111:1)
- "Therefore let us be grateful for receiving a kingdom that cannot be shaken, and thus let us offer to God acceptable worship, with reverence and awe, for our God is a consuming fire." (Hebrews 12:28-29)
- "For from his fullness we have all received, grace upon grace." (John 1:16)
- "[God] who saved us and called us to a holy calling, not because of our works but because of his own purpose and grace, which he gave us in Christ Jesus before the ages began." (2 Timothy 1:9)
- "And now I commend you to God and to the word of his grace, which is able to build you up and to give you the inheritance among all those who are sanctified." (Acts 20:32)
- "You then, my child, be strengthened by the grace that is in Christ Jesus." (2 Timothy 2:1)

Quick Prayers:

- "Lord, thank you for speaking to me."
- "Father, I am scared, but I know you are in control. Thank you for not abandoning me."
- "Lord, thank you for opening my eyes to your truth."
- "Father, I continue to surrender this to you. Thank you for the strength to move forward."
- "Lord, thank you for leading me as I capture every thought and test it to your will."

Closing Prayer:

"Father, thank you for being my Lord and Savior, never leaving my side, and guiding every step I take. I ask for your wisdom and understanding as I move forward through this journey. I praise you in advance for all you will accomplish in and through me as we navigate this trauma together. In Jesus' name, Amen."

Things to Try:

- Start a gratitude jar.
- Go on a gratitude walk.
- Write a letter of thanks to God.
- As you journal your prayers each day, begin by thanking God for something.

CHAPTER SIX

Step 4 of **S H I _F_ T** − Find

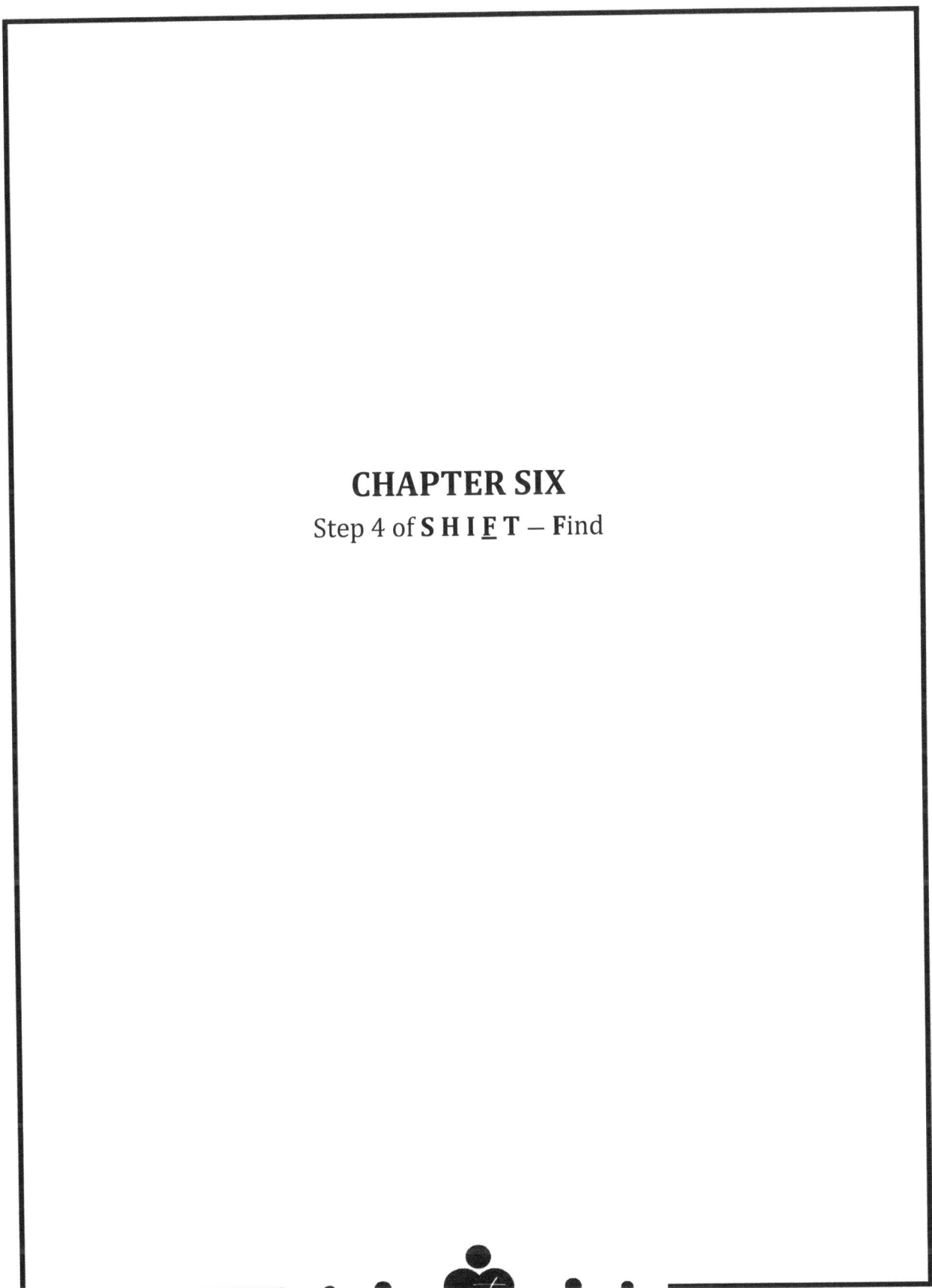

STEP 4 OF **SHIFT** – FIND

Action: Find Peace   **How:** Focus on the things Above   **Result:** Trust & Hope

ENTERING FREEDOM

As you continue through the **SHIFT** framework, you reach a turning point where God's next steps unfold naturally. When you shift your mindset in trauma, you walk in His will — seeking Him daily, immersing yourself in His Word, and cultivating gratitude for His presence and work in your life. As you move forward in faith, choosing obedience, extending forgiveness, practicing thankfulness, and embracing self-control, God gives you an incredible gift that no trauma or hardship can ever take away — His peace.

This peace is not just a breath of fresh air — it is like receiving an oxygen tank! The chaos that once consumed you is replaced with calm. The raging sea within you becomes still. This is a profound freedom, and once you experience it, you never want to live without it again.

The next step is finding peace, understanding that this step is not really an action step but rather an opportunity to embrace the peace Jesus brings. You cannot manufacture true peace or force it into your life. Instead, you experience it through an intimate, ongoing relationship with Jesus. It is a peace that defies all understanding — existing even before circumstances change. And now, you are living in it.

WHAT IS PEACE

As Scripture shows, peace is far more than the absence of conflict or a temporary sense of calm. Biblical peace is a deep, enduring sense of wholeness that flows from your relationship with God. **To find true peace is to find Jesus** — the Prince of Peace Himself. His presence brings rest to your soul, even in chaos.

This peace transcends your circumstances, offering you inner stillness and strength through God's presence and promises. Unlike the world's version of peace, which depends on everything going right around you, God's peace anchors and protects your heart and mind no matter what is happening externally.

Scripture describes peace in many ways: as a gift, a result of knowing God, and a fruit of the Spirit — evidence that He is alive and working within you.

Look up the following Scriptures and write out what stands out to you:

John 14:27: _____

_____

Romans 5:1: _____

_____

Galatians 5:22-23: _____

_____

_____

John 16:33:_____

_____

_____

Ephesians 2:14: _____

_____

_____

Matthew 6:31-34: _____

_____

_____

HOW DO I FIND PEACE

"And the peace of God, which surpasses all understanding, will guard your hearts and your minds in Christ Jesus." – Philippians 4:7

How do you find peace? You find Jesus – then peace comes.

How do you find Jesus? By focusing on the things above — setting your mind on Jesus rather than the distractions of this world (Colossians 3:2). When you seek Him first, His peace follows.

Peace is the result of a life centered on Jesus. It is not a temporary sense of relief but a divine gift that sustains you in every circumstance. It comes from trusting in God's presence, His promises, and His plan — not from external situations.

By aligning your life in these three areas, you can experience the peace only God provides, regardless of your circumstances.
- **Receive It** – Accept God's peace through faith by trusting His sovereignty, obeying His Word, and resting in His promises.
- **Live in It** – Walk in God's peace daily by seeking Him through prayer, focusing on His presence, and relying on the Holy Spirit.
- **Guard Your Mind** – Release anxiety and worry, renew your thoughts through forgiveness, and trust God's provision.

Read the following Scriptures and fill in the blanks:

 Receive It: Accepting God's Gift of Peace (Faith)
These steps focus on receiving God's peace as a gift and trusting in His promises.

- *Trust in God's Sovereignty*

Isaiah 26:3
"You keep him in perfect peace whose mind is stayed on you, because he trusts in you."

Peace comes when I trust God completely. Focusing my mind on His faithfulness brings

perfect _____.

- *Live in Obedience to God's Word*

John 14:23
"If anyone loves me, he will keep my word, and my Father will love him, and we will come to him and make our home with him."

Loving Jesus means keeping His _____, and when I do, I invite His_____ into my life.

- *Rest in the Assurance of God's Promise*

Romans 5:1
"Therefore, since we have been justified by faith, we have peace with God through our Lord Jesus Christ."

Journal:

_____

_____

_____

_____

_____

Live in It: Walking Daily in God's Peace (Trust)
These steps involve actively living in God's peace and trusting Him daily.

- *Seek God through Prayer*

Philippians 4:6-7
"Do not be anxious about anything, but in everything by prayer and supplication with thanksgiving let your requests be made known to God. And the peace of God, which surpasses all understanding, will guard your hearts and your minds in Christ Jesus."

Prayer is a key way to experience _____. Through_____, I hand over my anxieties to God

and receive peace in return.

- *Focus on God's Presence*

Psalm 16:11

"You make known to me the path of life; in your presence there is fullness of joy; at your right hand are pleasures forevermore."

Spending time in God's _____ through worship, prayer, and reflection fosters _____,

bringing joy and assurance.

- *Walk in the Holy Spirit*

Galatians 5:22-23

"But the fruit of the Spirit is love, joy, peace, forbearance, kindness, goodness, faithfulness, gentleness, self-control. Against such things there is no law."

As I walk in the _____, peace becomes a natural fruit of my life, helping me maintain calm and

composure through daily challenges.

Journal:

_____

_____

_____

_____

③ Guarding Your Mind: Reject Wrong-Minded Thinking

These steps involve rejecting anxiety, worry, and wrong thinking that hinder peace, and renewing your mind according to God's Word.

- *Release Worry and Anxiety*

Matthew 6:31-34

"Therefore do not be anxious, saying, 'What shall we eat?' or 'What shall we drink?' or 'What shall we wear?' ... But seek first the kingdom of God and his righteousness, and all these things will be added to you."

When I release my worry and _____, trusting God provides for me, He fills me with peace and

faithfully meets my needs.

- *Forgive and Let Go of Resentment*

Matthew 6:14-15

"For if you forgive others their trespasses, your heavenly Father will also forgive you, but if you do not forgive others their trespasses, neither will your Father forgive your trespasses."

Unforgiveness creates barriers to peace. When I choose to _____, I release resentment,

allowing peace to flow freely into my heart.

Journal:

_____

_____

_____

_____

_____

_____

_____

_____

God freely offers you the gift of peace, but you must choose to accept it and live in it. When you trust in His sovereignty, you embrace a steady peace — no matter your circumstances. The world's peace fades quickly, but God's peace endures because He is always in control.

THE RESULT OF FINDING PEACE

Finding peace results in trust and hope. Even in the midst of trauma and uncertainty, God's peace holds you steady. It reminds you that He is at work and will never leave your side. His peace anchors your soul and gives you the strength to keep going confidently, knowing His plan for you is good — no matter what you face.

Letting peace rule allows it to guide your thoughts, emotions, and actions. Living in peace does not mean you avoid challenges — it means you face them boldly, trusting that God is with you, He goes before you, and that His peace will guide you through every situation.

Read the following Scripture and fill in the blanks:

Romans 15:13
"May the God of hope fill you with all joy and peace in believing, so that by the power of the Holy Spirit you may abound in hope."

1. I will trust God to fill me with _____ and _____ as I believe in Him.

2. Through the power of the Holy Spirit, I will abound in _____.

PERSONAL APPLICATION

Finding and living in God's peace means receiving, walking in, and guarding the peace He offers. When we embrace His peace, we navigate trauma and triggers with confidence, knowing He is in control.

 Receive It: Accepting God's Gift of Peace (Faith)

Start by receiving the peace God freely gives. Jesus offers His peace to you personally in John 14:27:

"Peace I leave with you; my peace I give to you. Not as the world gives do I give to you. Let not your hearts be troubled, neither let them be afraid."

You choose to receive this peace when you trust God's sovereignty and surrender your fears and anxieties to Him. His peace is not temporary or dependent on your circumstances — it is a divine, unshakable calm that steadies you through life's storms. When you believe He is in control, you live in the peace only He can provide.

Am I open to receiving God's peace, or am I holding on to my fears and worries?

_____

_____

_____

_____

_____

_____

 Live in It: Walking Daily in God's Peace (Trust)

After you receive God's peace, choose to live in it. Make it a part of your daily walk. Living in peace means you do not just recognize it — you respond to life's challenges from a place of trust in God's protection and provision.

Colossians 3:15 urges you to let peace lead your life:

"And let the peace of Christ rule in your hearts, to which indeed you were called in one body. And be thankful."

Letting peace rule means giving it authority over your thoughts, emotions, and actions. You stay anchored by refusing to worry, turning to prayer instead, and resting in God's promises. Living in His peace does not mean you avoid hard things — it means you face them confidently, knowing God walks with you and His peace will lead you through every situation.

How can I allow God's peace to shape my response to stress, fear, or uncertainty?

_____

_____

_____

_____

_____

_____

_____

❸ *Guarding Your Mind: Reject Wrong-Minded Thinking*

Living in God's peace means actively rejecting wrong-minded thinking — the lies and distortions that lead to fear, anxiety, or doubt. The enemy constantly targets your thoughts, trying to steal your peace. But you take your stand by renewing your mind with the truth of God's Word.

Romans 12:2 gives you this clear command:

"Do not be conformed to this world, but be transformed by the renewal of your mind, that by testing you may discern what is the will of God, what is good and acceptable and perfect."

You guard your peace by filling your mind with truth. You recognize and reject lies by meditating on Scripture, capturing every thought (2 Corinthians 10:5), and standing firm in the truth that God remains in control.

Philippians 4:8 gives us a clear guide for what we should focus on:

"Finally, brothers, whatever is true, whatever is honorable, whatever is just, whatever is pure, whatever is lovely, whatever is commendable, if there is any excellence, if there is anything worthy of praise, think about these things."

When you train your mind to focus on truth and praise, you open the door to the fullness of God's peace.

What negative thought patterns do I need to reject to experience more of God's peace in my life?

_____

_____

_____

_____

Additional Personal Application Questions for Journaling:

- How can I actively receive and embrace God's peace in my daily life?
- What steps can I take to ensure that I live in peace rather than allowing fear or anxiety to rule my heart?
- What thought patterns must I reject or renew to walk fully in God's peace?
- What areas of my life do I need to trust God more deeply?
- How can I acknowledge God more in the areas where I struggle to trust Him?

Journal:

_____

_____

_____

_____

_____

_____

_____

_____

_____

_____

_____

_____

_____

_____

_____

_____

_____

_____

_____

_____

_____

ADDITIONAL RESOURCES

<u>Memory Verses:</u>
- "Surely he has borne our griefs and carried our sorrows; yet we esteemed him stricken, smitten by God, and afflicted. But he was pierced for our transgressions; he was crushed for our iniquities; upon him was the chastisement that brought us peace, and with his wounds we are healed." (Isaiah 53:4-5)
- "The Lord is my shepherd; I shall not want. He makes me lie down in green pastures. He leads me beside still waters. He restores my soul." (Psalm 23:1-3)
- "The Lord is my strength and my shield; in him my heart trusts, and I am helped." (Psalm 28:7)
- "The Lord gives strength to his people; the Lord blesses his people with peace." (Psalm 29:11)
- "Commit your way to the Lord; trust in him, and he will act." (Psalm 37:5)
- "Come to me, all who labor and are heavy laden, and I will give you rest." (Matthew 11:28)
- "Set your minds on things that are above, not on things that are on earth." (Colossians 3:2)
- "Let the peace of Christ rule in your hearts, to which indeed you were called in one body." (Colossians 3:15)
- "For God gave us a spirit not of fear but of power and love and self-control." (2 Timothy 1:7)
- "But this I call to mind, and therefore I have hope: The steadfast love of the Lord never ceases; his mercies never come to an end; they are new every morning; great is your faithfulness." (Lamentations 3:21-23)
- "The Lord is near to all who call on him, to all who call in him in truth. He fulfills the desires of those who fear him; he also hears their cry and saves them." (Psalm 145:18-21)
- "Be still, and know that I am God. I will be exalted among the nations, I will be exalted in the earth!" (Psalm 46:10)
- "Blessed is the man who trusts in the Lord, whose trust is the Lord." (Jeremiah 17:7)
- "For God alone, O my soul, wait in silence, for my hope is from him. He only is my rock and my salvation, my fortress; I shall not be shaken." (Psalm 62:5-6)
- "Now may the Lord of peace himself give you peace at all times in every way. The Lord be with you all." (2 Thessalonians 3:16)

<u>Quick Prayers:</u>
- "Lord, fill my heart with your peace that surpasses all understanding."
- "Father, teach me how to stay focused on you."
- "Lord, remind me of your presence and fill me with unwavering peace and trust."
- "Father, help me trust you more deeply in every situation."
- "Lord, strengthen my hope in your promises and your perfect plan for my life."

<u>Closing Prayer:</u>
"Lord, I thank you for the gift of your peace. Help me to receive it fully, to live in it daily, and to reject any thoughts or lies that try to steal it from me. I trust your peace will guard my heart and mind in every situation. In Jesus' name, Amen."

<u>Things to Try:</u>
- Take a walk in nature.
- Practice breathing while quiet — set a 5 minutes timer for simply being with God.
- Journal the triggers you face and how God is helping you find peace and purpose through them.
- Write a letter to God about what you are carrying and how you want to trust Him.

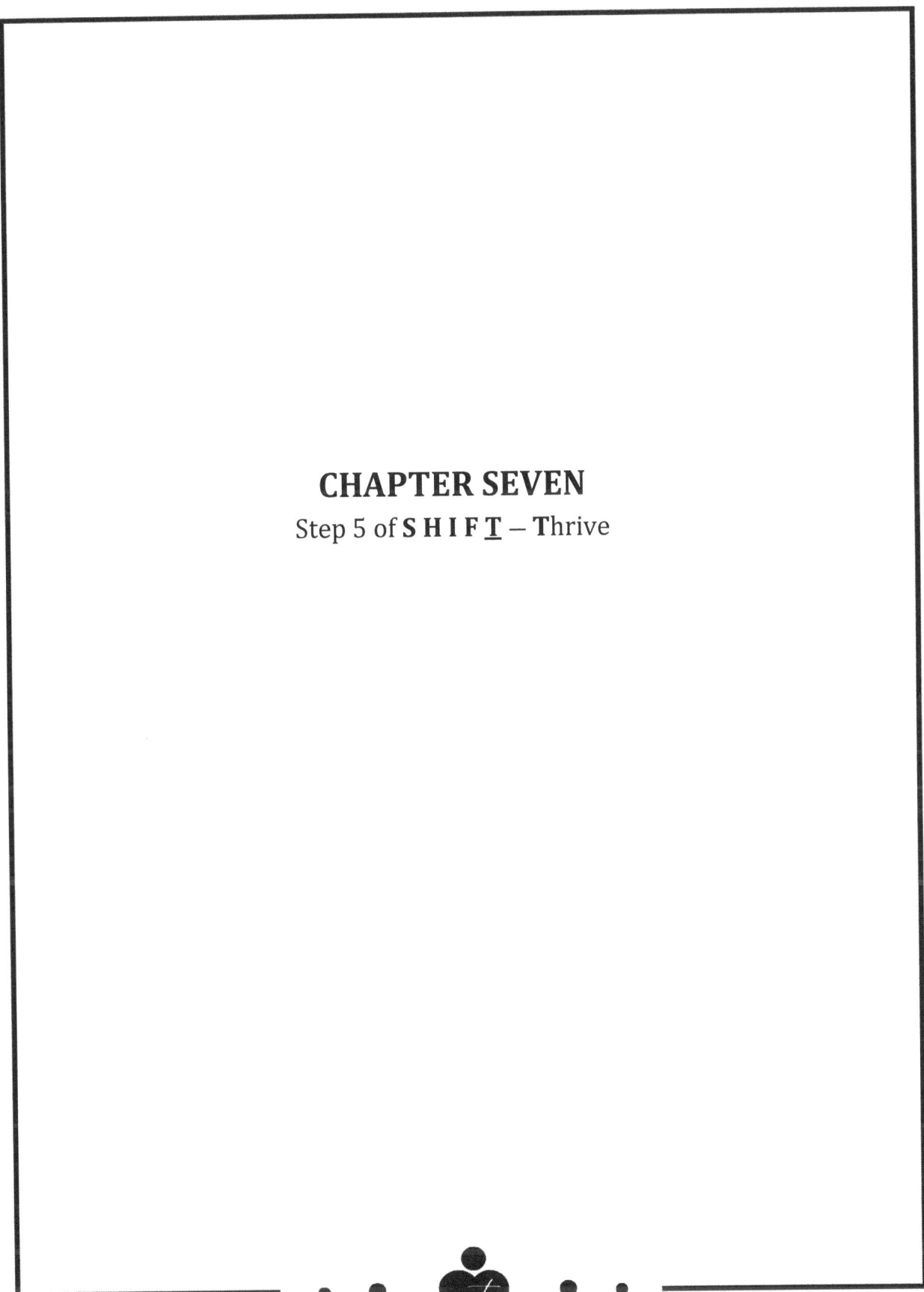

CHAPTER SEVEN
Step 5 of **S H I F <u>T</u>** – **T**hrive

STEP 5 OF **SHIF̲T** – **T**HRIVE

Action: Thrive in God's Presence　**How:** Trust His Process　**Result:** Praise & Purpose

JUST SURVIVING

Surviving trauma takes everything you have. It demands grit and endurance to get through the day when your world feels shattered and uncertain. Every step feels heavy. Some moments, you wonder if you can even keep going. But survival is not the end of your story — it is the starting point.

Thriving through trauma reveals your resilience. It is a powerful testimony of what happens when you lean into your faith, trust God's plan, and refuse to give up — especially on the hardest days.

WHAT DOES IT MEAN TO THRIVE

"I have fought the good fight, I have finished the race, I have kept the faith." – 2 Timothy 4:7

The **SHIFT** framework begins with a decision — will you walk in the flesh or walk in the Spirit?

The wide path of the flesh often feels easier — especially in seasons of deep hurt. It offers quick relief, false comfort, and temporary distractions that numb but never heal. That road leads to survival mode — hiding behind bitterness, self-medicating, and exhaustion. You may still be standing, but you are not truly living.

The Spirit invites you onto a different path — narrower, quieter, and not always easy. But this is the path where profound transformation begins. On this path, you stop running from your pain and start meeting God right in the middle of it. You do not wait for life to get easier to believe — you lean in and let faith rise. You trust God's promises. You rest in His timing. And even when the tears keep pouring out, you open your heart to His presence.

Your trust deepens as you continue to choose Him in the hard places. You begin to grow — not despite the trial but through it. Gratitude replaces grumbling. Hope begins to rise again. You stop striving for control and surrender to the One who already holds the outcome. Thriving in God's presence means staying spiritually rooted, emotionally grounded, and mentally renewed. You begin to live not from your own strength, but from the strength He supplies.

To thrive means you choose trust over control. You choose surrender over striving. You choose peace over panic — not because the storm disappears, but because you are held by the One who commands the winds and waves.

"Faith never knows where it is being led, but it loves and knows the One who is leading."

- Oswald Chambers

Read the following Scriptures and reflect:

Romans 5:2-5
"Through him we have also obtained access by faith into this grace in which we stand, and we rejoice in hope of the glory of God. Not only that, but we rejoice in our sufferings, knowing that suffering produces endurance, and endurance produces character, and character produces hope, and hope does not put us to shame, because God's love has been poured into our hearts through the Holy Spirit who has been given to us."

Isaiah 40:31
"But they who wait for the Lord shall renew their strength; they shall mount up with wings like eagles; they shall run and not be weary; they shall walk and not faint."

Matthew 5:14-16
"You are the light of the world. A city set on a hill cannot be hidden. Nor do people light a lamp and put it under a basket, but on a stand, and it gives light to all in the house. In the same way, let your light shine before others, so that they may see your good works and give glory to your Father who is in heaven."

What stands out to you from the above passages? _____

_____

_____

_____

_____

What would thriving look like in your current season? _____

_____

_____

_____

_____

How can you rely on God's strength this week? _____

_____

_____

_____

HOW DO I THRIVE

You thrive in God's presence when you actively trust His process. When you release control and fully surrender your life to God you show that you trust His authority over every part of your life. You do not need to have all the answers or understand every step. Instead, you loosen your grip on your plans and allow God to lead you. You invite His presence to heal, guide, and transform — with open hands and a willing heart.

Healing may come slowly, and some days may feel like setbacks. But moving from surviving to thriving begins when you trust God through it all. It is choosing to honor Him with your choices and your life. Your attitude becomes an offering. Your obedience becomes worship. You trust His timing and His wisdom, honoring Him by walking forward in faith — even when the path is unclear.

Peter experienced trust firsthand. In the middle of the storm, Jesus called him to come. Peter walked on water toward Him — faith enabled the impossible! But the moment he looked at the waves instead of the Savior, fear took over and he began to sink. Still, Jesus immediately reached out and rescued him (Matthew 14:28–31). Thriving is not about perfection — it is about connection. You lay down fear and pick up faith. You stop striving and start abiding. You let His Spirit lead, comfort, correct, and heal.

As you walk this narrow path (Matthew 7:14), you begin to rest — not because everything is calm, but because you know the One who offers you rest. Fear no longer controls your decisions. Peace replaces pressure. Hope grows resilient. You no longer deny your pain — and you no longer face it alone. God walks with you through every high and every low, using even suffering to deepen your connection with Him.

Thriving is more than healing — it is becoming. You begin to live with courage, sleep with peace, and trust that God's hand is over your future. Your life becomes a light that shows others that healing is possible. You no longer survive, you thrive — fully alive, grounded in purpose, and transformed by the presence of a God who never leaves. Your story becomes a living testimony of His faithfulness, hope, and grace.

Look up the following Scriptures and fill in the blanks:

Proverbs 3:5-6

"Trust in the Lord with all your heart, and do not lean on your own _____. In all your

ways _____ Him, and He will make straight your paths."

Isaiah 55:8-9

"For my _____ are not your thoughts, neither are your ways my_____ , declares

the Lord. For as the heavens are higher than the earth, so are my ways higher than your ways and my

thoughts than your thoughts."

Matthew 19:26

"But Jesus looked at them and said, 'With man this is_____ , but with God things are possible.'"

Ephesians 3:20

"Now to him who is able to do far more abundantly than all that we _____ or_____ , according to the power at work within us..."

How can I rejoice and praise Him even in uncertainty?

_____

_____

_____

_____

What step can I take today to fully trust Him and thrive in His presence?

_____

_____

_____

_____

THE RESULT OF THRIVING

"Let everything that has breath praise the Lord! Praise the Lord!" – Psalm 150:6

The result of thriving is a life marked by praise and purpose. Thriving in the middle of trauma and triggers is not just about making it through — it is about meeting God in the mess and lifting your voice in worship, even before answers come. You celebrate His presence before the breakthrough and honor Him with trust while waiting.

Praise becomes a posture, not just a song — the posture of a soft heart. It shifts your focus from what feels broken to the One who heals. Choosing worship over worry silences fear, invites peace, and anchors your soul in hope — something impossible with a hardened heart. Rejoicing does not deny pain — it declares who God is in the middle of it. Worship in the waiting proclaims that your God is greater than the storm. Faith deepens, peace replaces pressure, and hope strengthens in this place.

As you thrive, your healing becomes a testimony. You begin to see your journey is not just for you — it is for others who need to see that God still restores. You walk forward not in your own strength, but in His.

This kind of thriving rejoices in the storm because it trusts the One who commands it. Your peace is no longer tied to your circumstances — it is grounded in the presence of the God who is faithful, even in the unknown.

The disciples once asked, "What sort of man is this, that even winds and sea obey Him?" (Matthew 8:27). That same Jesus — who calmed the storm, fed the multitudes, and conquered the grave — is holding your life now.

If He commands the waves, He also speaks over your healing. Nothing escapes His care. You can trust His heart, even when you do not understand His hand. He is present, He is working, and He is faithful.

Look up the following Scriptures and fill in the blanks:

Philippians 4:4
"Rejoice in the Lord_____; again I will say,_____!"

James 1:2-4
"Count it all_____, my brothers, when you meet trials of various kinds, for you know that the testing

of your faith produces steadfastness. And let _____have its full effect, that you may be

perfect and complete, lacking in nothing."

Read Psalm 100 and journal your thoughts:

_____

_____

_____

_____

_____

_____

_____

_____

_____

_____

PERSONAL APPLICATION

Praise in the waiting transforms your perspective. It breaks the grip of anxiety, aligns your heart with God's truth, and moves you from surviving to thriving. By trusting His process, you declare His faithfulness and lean into His purpose — even when it is not yet clear.

So lift your eyes. Praise while you wait. Learn to rest, even while the storm rages, because your peace no longer depends on your circumstances — it rests in the One who commands them. This is the posture of thriving — trusting the process, surrendering the outcome, and worshiping the God who walks with you through it all.

Look up and read the following Scriptures. Write down the verse or what stands out to you:

 Choose Praise Over Anxiety:
Shift your focus from fear to faith by praising God in every situation.

Philippians 4:6-7: _____

_____

_____

1 Peter 5:7: _____

_____

_____

Align Your Heart with God's Truth:
Let Scripture and prayer ground you in His sovereignty and goodness.

Psalm 119:105: _____

_____

_____

Psalm 34:1: _____

_____

_____

3 *Trust His Timing and Process:*
Replace impatience with faith, knowing He is always at work.

Exodus 14:14: _____

_____

_____

Psalm 27:14: _____

_____

_____

4 *Seek God's Purpose in the Pain:*
Ask Him to reveal how He is using your struggles for growth and healing.

2 Corinthians 4:17-18: _____

_____

_____

Isaiah 43:2: _____

_____

_____

5 *Share Your Testimony:*
Let your praise be a witness to God's faithfulness and encourage others in their journey.

Psalm 66:16: _____

_____

_____

1 Chronicles 16:8: _____

_____

_____

How can I shift my focus from anxiety to praise in my current circumstances?

_____

_____

_____

What truths from the Scriptures can I regularly remind myself to align my heart with God's will during this waiting period?

_____

_____

_____

What can I learn from the pain or challenges I am experiencing, and how can I seek God's purpose in them?

_____

_____

_____

What areas of my life am I holding onto instead of surrendering to God?

_____

_____

_____

Journal:

_____

_____

_____

_____

_____

_____

_____

ADDITIONAL RESOURCES

<u>Memory Verses:</u>
- "And those who know your name put their trust in you, for you, O Lord, have not forsaken those who seek you. Sing praises to the Lord, who sits enthroned in Zion! Tell among the peoples his deeds!" (Psalm 9:11)
- "You make known to me the path of life. In your presence there is fullness of joy; at your right hand are pleasures forevermore." (Psalm 16:11)
- "Commit your way to the Lord; trust in him, and he will act." (Psalm 37:5)
- "But I will sing of your strength; I will sing aloud of your steadfast love in the morning. For you have been to me a fortress and a refuge in the day of my distress. O my Strength, I will sing praises to you, for you, O God, are my fortress, the God who shows me steadfast love." (Psalm 59:16-17)
- "From the rising of the sun to its setting, the name of the Lord is to be praised!" (Psalm 113:3)
- "Humble yourselves before the Lord, and he will exalt you." (James 4:10)
- "Rejoice in the Lord always; again I will say, rejoice." (Philippians 4:4)
- "Rejoice always, pray without ceasing, give thanks in all circumstances; for this is the will of God in Christ Jesus for you." (1 Thessalonians 5:15-16)
- "Therefore let us be grateful for receiving a kingdom that cannot be shaken, and thus let us offer to God acceptable worship, with reverence and awe." (Hebrews 12:28)
- "Rejoice in hope, be patient in tribulation, be constant in prayer." (Romans 12:12)
- "Therefore let those who suffer according to God's will entrust their souls to a faithful Creator while doing good." (1 Peter 4:19)

<u>Quick Prayers:</u>
- "Lord, help me shift my focus from anxiety to praise, trusting that you are in control of every circumstance."
- "Father, teach me to align my heart with your truth and to praise you in all seasons of life continuously."
- "Lord, remind me of your presence and help me trust your timing and process, even when I can't see the full picture."
- "Father, deepen my trust in you, especially when I face challenges, and help me see your purpose in the waiting."
- "Lord, strengthen my hope in your promises and empower me to share your faithfulness with others."

<u>Closing Prayer:</u>
"Lord, thank You for Your peace that surpasses all understanding. Help me to embrace it fully, live with it daily, and reject any anxiety or doubt that tries to take it away. May your peace guard my heart and mind as I trust your perfect plan and purpose in every situation. I commit to praising you through every season, knowing you are always at work for my good. In Jesus' name, Amen."

<u>Things to Try:</u>
- Find a Church for community and worship
- Start a new playlist – Healing Songs
- Use an affirmations book or start an affirmations journal

CHAPTER EIGHT
Applying **SHIFT** in Daily Life

APPLYING SHIFT IN DAILY LIFE

FROM REACTION TO TRANSFORMATION

The **SHIFT** framework helps you transform your natural reactions and set your mind on things above (Colossians 3:2), aligning your perspective with God's truth. When you shift your mindset, you stop reacting from fear, anger, or pain and start responding with faith, hope, and trust in God's promises.

As you adjust how you view your circumstances, emotions, and healing process, you make space for God's transforming power to work in you. This shift impacts both how fast and how deeply you heal. Instead of being consumed by pain, you begin to see it through a lens of faith and hope.

You realize healing is not just physical or emotional — it is profoundly spiritual and rooted in your relationship with God. Use these steps daily to strengthen your shift in mindset as you walk through your journey of healing and restoration.

SHIFT FRAMEWORK
A Biblical Approach to Mindset Transformation for Healing and Resilience

SURRENDER

Action: Surrender to God's Plan
How: Pray — Choose to let go of control and surrender your burdens, struggles, past, present, and future to God through prayer. Start talking to Him.
Result: Faith & Obedience
Scripture: Philippians 4:6 — "Do not be anxious about anything, but in everything by prayer and supplication with thanksgiving let your requests be made known to God." Jeremiah 29:11-13 — "For I know the plans I have for you, declares the LORD, plans for welfare and not for evil, to give you a future and a hope. Then you will call upon me and come and pray to me, and I will hear you. You will seek me and find me, when you seek me with all your heart."
Journal: Prayers

HEAR

Action: Hear God's Voice
How: Be in the Word — Reflect and test everything to the spirit, ensuring alignment with God's truth by being in the Word and taking every thought captive.
Result: Humility & Thanksgiving
Scripture: 1 John 4:1 — "Beloved, do not believe every spirit, but test the spirits to see whether they are from God, for many false prophets have gone out into the world." Romans 10:17 — "So faith comes from hearing, and hearing through the word of Christ." John 1:1 — "In the beginning was the Word, and the Word was with God, and the Word was God."
Journal: Dreams

INVITE IN

Action: Invite in God's Grace
How: Through Gratitude — Cultivate a heart of gratitude, appreciating God's blessings despite circumstances by living in Thanksgiving.
Result: Self-Control & Peace
Scripture: 1 Thessalonians 5:18 — "Give thanks in all circumstances; for this is the will of God in Christ Jesus for you." Philippians 4:6 — "Do not be anxious about anything, but in everything by prayer and supplication with thanksgiving let your requests be made known to God."
Journal: Thanksgiving/Gratitude

FIND

Action: Find Peace (in Jesus)
How: Focus on the things Above — Become set free from worries and burdens by the peace that transcends understanding when you focus on the things above.
Result: Trust & Hope
Scripture: Philippians 4:7-9 — "And the peace of God, which surpasses all understanding, will guard your hearts and your minds in Christ Jesus. Finally, brothers, whatever is true, whatever is honorable, whatever is just, whatever is pure, whatever is lovely, whatever is commendable, if there is any excellence, if there is anything worthy of praise, think about these things. What you have learned and received and heard and seen in me — practice these things, and the God of peace will be with you." John 14:27 NLT — "I am leaving you with a gift — peace of mind and heart. And the peace I give is a gift the world cannot give. So don't be troubled or afraid." Colossians 3:2 — "Set your minds on things that are above, not on things that are on earth."
Journal: Peace/Purpose

THRIVE

Action: Thrive in God's Presence
How: Trust His Process — Rejoice with joy and praise, celebrating God's faithfulness through outward worship and inward surrender.
Result: Praise & Purpose
Scripture: Philippians 4:4 — "Rejoice in the Lord always; again I will say, rejoice." Romans 5:2-5 — "Through him we have also obtained access by faith into this grace in which we stand, and we rejoice in hope of the glory of God. Not only that, but we rejoice in our sufferings, knowing that suffering produces endurance, and endurance produces character, and character produces hope, and hope does not put us to shame, because God's love has been poured into our hearts through the Holy Spirit who has been given to us."
Journal: Worship Playlist

PHILIPPIANS 4:4-9

Rejoice in the Lord always; again I will say, rejoice. Let your reasonableness be known to everyone. The Lord is at hand; do not be anxious about anything, but in everything by prayer and supplication with thanksgiving let your requests be made known to God. And the peace of God, which surpasses all understanding, will guard your hearts and your minds in Christ Jesus. Finally, brothers, whatever is true, whatever is honorable, whatever is just, whatever is pure, whatever is lovely, whatever is commendable, if there is any excellence, if there is anything worthy of praise, think about these things. What you have learned and received and heard and seen in me — practice these things, and the God of peace will be with you.

Surrender to God's Plan: PRAY

Hear God's Voice: BE IN THE WORD

Invite in God's Grace: ATTITUDE OF GRATITUDE

Find Peace in Jesus: FOCUS ON THINGS ABOVE

Thrive in God's Presence: WORSHIP

WWW.MINDSETMATTERSCOMMUNICATIONS.COM

CHAPTER NINE
The Bible and Our Body – **REST** FRAMEWORK

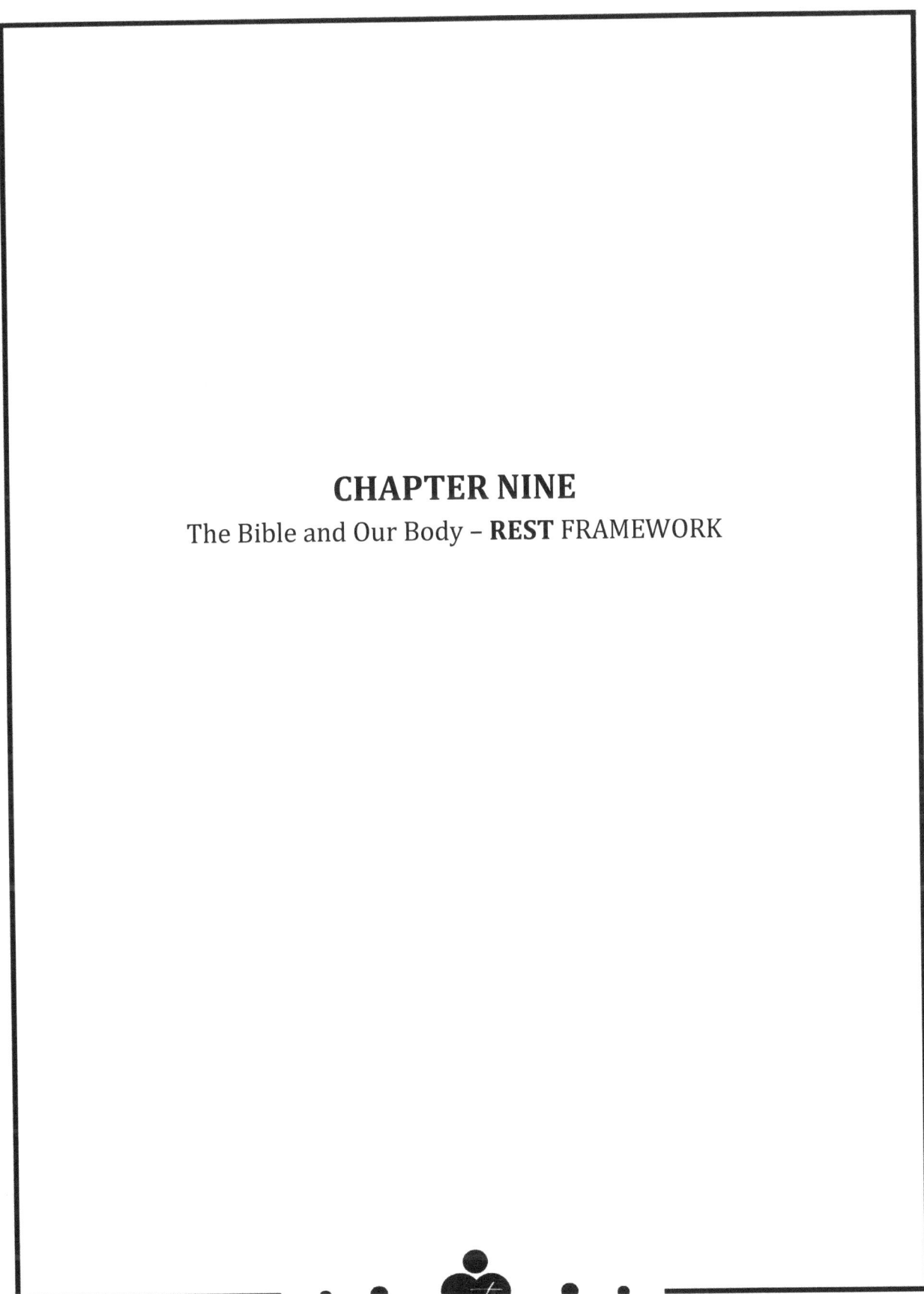

THE BIBLE AND OUR BODY

REST FRAMEWORK

Multiple Scriptures describe our bodies' role and impact, with one of the most well-known truths being that our bodies are a temple of God (1 Corinthians 6:19-20). To truly love God with all our heart, soul, and mind (Matthew 22:37), we must expand on what we have learned about mindset by developing awareness of our whole being — this is **SOMATIC AWARENESS**.

Trauma often disconnects us from our bodies and clouds our thinking, making it challenging to engage with faith, hope, and love fully. Somatic awareness is simply the ability to recognize and attune to how trauma, stress, and healing manifest in our bodies, allowing us to reconnect with ourselves and God.

When we intentionally **SHIFT** our mindset toward God, we invite Him to transform our hearts and minds, leading us into more profound healing and a closer relationship with Him. Likewise, when we learn to **REST** in His presence, we allow Him to renew our bodies, bringing restoration from the inside out.

As you engage with these exercises, you will learn practical ways to regulate your body, using them as a tool to draw nearer to God, no matter what circumstances you face.

You will notice mentions of the body in these passages. Write them out and underline what stands out to you:

Proverbs 14:30: _____

_____

Job 4:14: _____

_____

_____

2 Corinthians 4:16: _____

_____

_____

Psalm 32:3-4: _____

_____

_____

_____

Romans 12:1-2: _____

_____

_____

_____

_____

Mark 5:29-30: _____

_____

_____

_____

Reflect on what you have learned about the importance of your body from these Scriptures. Which verses stood out to you most and why?

_____

_____

_____

_____

_____

_____

_____

What did you find encouraging and hopeful from dwelling on these passages?

_____

_____

_____

_____

_____

_____

_____

_____

_____

_____

_____

_____

_____

_____

_____

_____

_____

_____

_____

PRACTICAL STEPS WITH THE REST FRAMEWORK

To cultivate a way to regulate ourselves when our nervous system gets hijacked during trauma, we must not only learn the practical steps outlined in the following chapters but also commit to remembering and applying them. Despite the circumstances, resting in God's presence is not a one-time task — rather, it is a deliberate process of retraining our somatic habits. This daily practice reshapes the subconscious, enabling us to thrive through and beyond life-altering events.

The steps are organized into the acronym **REST** to make learning and applying these principles more manageable during trauma.

REST

The **REST** framework helps us cultivate somatic awareness, which allows us to connect with our body's signals and use those insights to process and heal from trauma, stress, and emotional burdens. Through **REST**, we learn to trade our weariness and burdens for peace and restoration, resting in God's presence (Matthew 11:28-29)

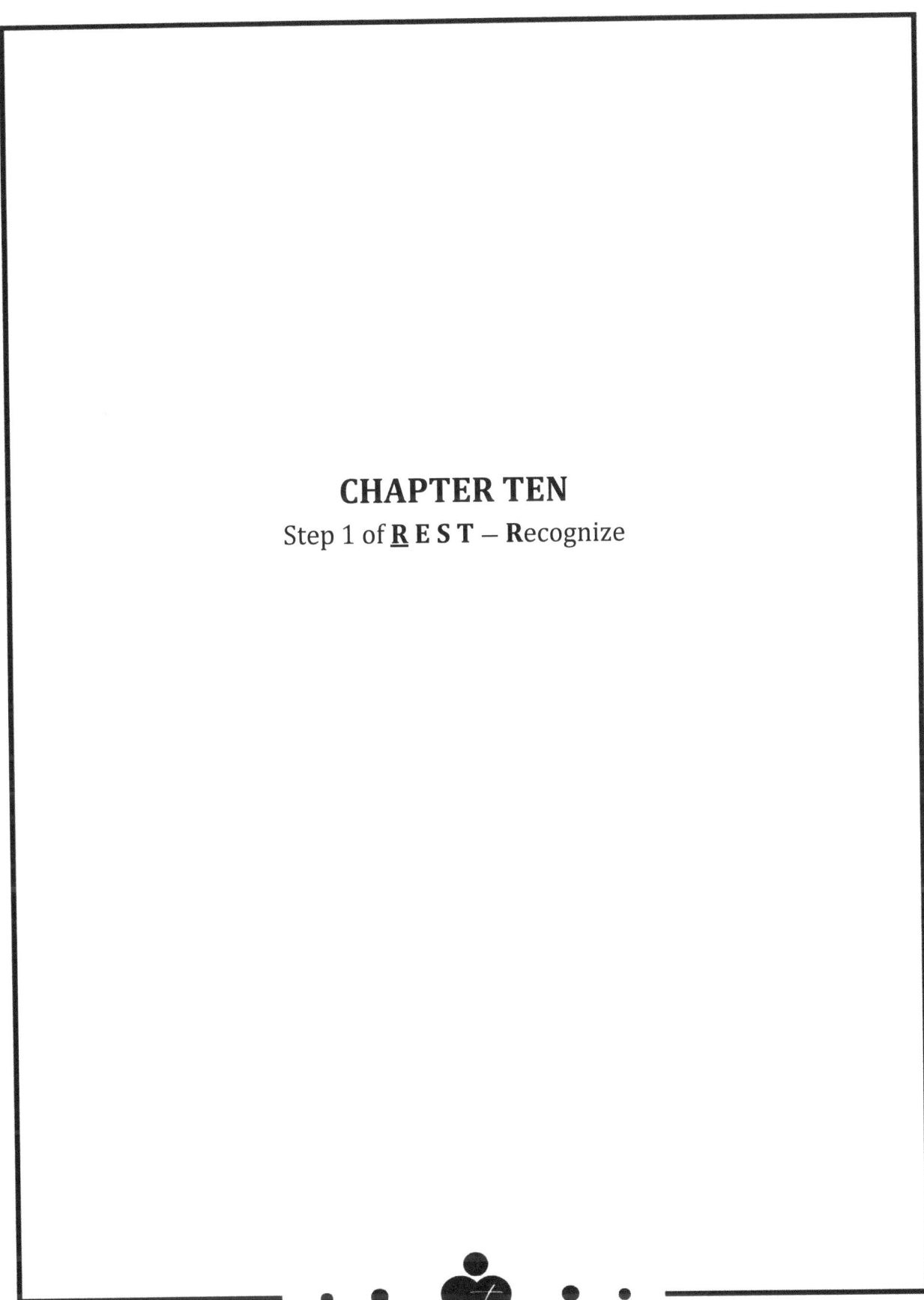

CHAPTER TEN
Step 1 of **R** E S T – **R**ecognize

STEP 1 OF **REST** – RECOGNIZE

Action: Recognize
How: Identify the body's signals in the moment – Name it
Result: Release the weight of trauma to God

DO NOT OVERLOOK THIS

When you walk the path of surrender with your mindset shifted upward, it is crucial not to overlook the physical burdens your body carries during trauma and healing. Ignoring the somatic side of trauma keeps you trapped in a loop where unprocessed emotions get stored in your body, leading to long-term health issues, recurring struggles, and even shifts in your personality. Breaking this cycle starts with recognizing and engaging with the body's signals during trauma and triggers. This intentional step is key to experiencing true healing and lasting peace in your soul and body.

WHAT DOES IT MEAN TO RECOGNIZE

This first step of **REST** is so crucial for complete mind and body healing. **To recognize means becoming aware of what is happening in your body in the present moment** — this is your **Felt Sense.** When you ignore your body's signals and your brain stays stuck in fight, flight, freeze, or fawn mode (Appendix A, page 113), you remain trapped in a cycle of stress, unable to regulate your nervous system — that is trauma. But when you recognize and acknowledge your pain, you invite God into that space. He is near to the brokenhearted and ready to bring healing and peace.

Read the following Scripture:

Psalm 34:18
"The Lord is near to the brokenhearted and saves the crushed in spirit."

How does this verse challenge/comfort you as you begin to recognize your body's response to trauma?

_____

_____

_____

_____

_____

_____

_____

HOW DO I RECOGNIZE

"Come to me, all who labor and are heavy laden, and I will give you rest. Take my yoke upon you, and learn from me, for I am gentle and lowly in heart, and you will find rest for your souls."
— *Matthew 11:28-29*

Recognize your somatic responses by identifying the signals your body is sending. When facing trauma or triggers, pause and take control of your environment. Stop everything you are doing when you can, and create a safe and comfortable space. Do you need quiet and darkness? Turn off all distractions and dim the lights. If music helps, put on worship songs that soothe your Spirit. Then, find your position — whether sitting, lying on your back, face down, or in any other position that feels right for you. Once settled, move through the following steps:

1. Set the Environment and Pause — Set up a comfortable and safe environment. Take a deep breath and remain still. By pausing and breathing, you are allowing your nervous system to reset and create space for awareness instead of reacting impulsively.

2. Scan Your Body — Close your eyes and identify where you feel tension, heaviness, or discomfort.

3. Name It — Describe your body's signals: Is it tight, heavy, warm, cold, shaky, or numb? See the Personal Applications section on page 75 for a list of signals.

4. Bring It to God — Acknowledge what you feel in prayer, describing it to Him.

As you recognize and bring these signals to God, how do you feel His presence in your body? Do you sense His comfort or peace entering into those areas of tension?

_____

_____

_____

_____

_____

_____

The Old Testament contains many stories of God's people crying out to Him, acknowledging the weight they carried, and God responded. King David writes in Psalm 34:17, "When the righteous cry for help, the Lord hears and delivers them out of all their troubles."

Read the following Scriptures and fill in the blanks:

Psalm 139:23-24 (NIV)
"Search me, God, and know my heart; test me and know my anxious thoughts. See if there is any offensive way in me, and lead me in the way everlasting."

Lamentations 3:19-22 (NLT)
"The thought of my suffering and homelessness is bitter beyond words. I will never forget this awful time, as I grieve over my loss. Yet I still dare to hope when I remember this: The faithful love of the Lord never ends! His mercies never cease."

Psalm 42:5 (NIV)
"Why, my soul, are you downcast? Why so disturbed within me? Put your hope in God, for I will yet praise him, my Savior and my God."

Job 30:16 (NIV)
"And now my life ebbs away; days of suffering grip me."

Psalm 6:6-9 (NLT)
"I am worn out from sobbing. All night I flood my bed with weeping, drenching it with my tears. My vision is blurred by grief; my eyes are worn out because of all my enemies. Go away, all you who do evil, for the Lord has heard my weeping. The Lord has heard my plea; the Lord will answer my prayer."

1. From the Scriptures above, what emotions, feelings, or actions are mentioned that reflect pain, grief, or sorrow?

The emotions highlighted in these Scriptures include _____, _____, and _____.

2. In the midst of suffering and grief, what key reminder or hope do the Scriptures provide about God's character?

Scriptures remind us that God's _____ never ends, and He is faithful to _____ my prayers.

These Scriptures show that even biblical figures like Job openly recognized their pain and suffering before God. Ask God to reveal what you are feeling in your body and Spirit. Recognizing pain is part of healing — yet God's love remains constant. God hears and responds when you acknowledge and express your emotions to Him.

THE RESULT OF RECOGNIZING

By pausing to recognize and intentionally acknowledge what your body is experiencing, you begin to release the weight of trauma to God. Instead of suppressing or ignoring these feelings, you allow healing to begin, knowing that God sees your pain and is near to comfort you.

Read the Scriptures and fill in the blanks:

Psalm 55:22
"Cast your burden on the Lord, and he will sustain you; he will never permit the righteous to be moved."

1. When I cast my burdens on the Lord, He will _____ me.

2. He will keep the righteous from being _____.

Isaiah 41:10
"Fear not, for I am with you; be not dismayed, for I am your God; I will strengthen you, I will help you, I will uphold you with my righteous right hand."

1. I am commanded to _____ not because God is with me.

2. He promises to _____, _____, and _____ me with His righteous right hand.

PERSONAL APPLICATION

Journaling is a powerful tool, especially when it focuses on healing with the help of the **REST** framework. Recognizing and acknowledging the signals your body is experiencing connects you to the Felt Sense, which opens up the door to engaging in these feelings in order to begin healing them. Feel free to use your journal or the journaling space on the next page.

Here is a list of possible signals of stress or anxiety caused by trauma or triggers that can manifest in your body. Circle the ones you are experiencing now, and underline the ones you have experienced before:

Teeth grinding or jaw clenching

Tightly clenched buttocks or pelvic tension

Constant frowning or scowling

Racing or pounding heart

Tension headaches or migraines

Shoulder or neck stiffness

Stomach issues like nausea, cramps, or diarrhea

Shortness of breath or shallow breathing

Sweating excessively, especially on palms/face

Trembling or shaky hands

Fatigue or extreme tiredness

Muscle twitches or spasms

Restlessness or inability to sit still

Tightness in the chest or difficulty breathing deeply

Dry mouth or frequent swallowing

Gripping objects harder than necessary

Tingling or numbness in extremities

Frequent urination or changes in bladder habits

Sudden weight loss or gain

Appetite changes

Skin breakouts or rashes

Hair thinning or loss

Frequent sighing or deep breaths

Cold or clammy hands and feet

Trouble falling asleep or staying asleep

Journal — Do the following exercises:

- Take a few minutes today to be still and recognize what your body is holding.
- Notice any physical signals, where you feel them, and what emotions or actions might be connected. Journal what you experience and pray through it.
- Meditate on Psalm 34:18 and invite God to meet you in your brokenness.
- As you go through the day, practice noticing when your body reacts to stress or emotions and intentionally giving those moments to God.
- Create a **REST** journal to track your somatic awareness progress.
- See the checklist below to guide you as you track your progress.

RECOGNIZE + RECORD CHECKLIST

Step	Notes / Reflections
❏ Pause for 3–5 minutes of stillness	What physical sensations do I notice?
❏ Identify where in my body I feel them	E.g., tight chest, clenched jaw, heavy shoulders
❏ Name the connected emotion or thought	What does this remind me of? What emotion or thought is present?
❏ Recognize the possible trigger	What situation, memory, or thought sparked this reaction?
❏ Pray through the sensation	What do I want to say to God right now?
❏ Surrender or invite God in	How can I invite God's presence into this moment?
❏ Write down any insights or patterns	What stands out as important to remember or notice next time?

Journal:

_____

_____

_____

_____

_____

_____

_____

_____

_____

_____

CHAPTER ELEVEN
Step 2 of R **E** S T — Engage

STEP 2 OF **REST** – ENGAGE

Action: Engage
How: Connect with the Felt Sense and remain present with the physical experience –
Use grounding techniques
Result: Embrace God's presence and promises

THE FELT SENSE?

As you recall from the beginning of this workbook, **trauma is an emotional response to a life-altering or deeply distressing event.** It occurs when an event's impact overwhelms your mental ability to cope, often leaving you feeling helpless, unsafe, or unable to regain a sense of normalcy – leading to an unregulated nervous system. The Felt Sense is your body's way of communicating deep, unspoken emotions and experiences. It is the physical awareness of what you are holding inside — tension, warmth, heaviness, or a stirring sensation that signals something unresolved. Rather than ignoring or suppressing these feelings, engaging with the Felt Sense allows you to stay present and move toward healing.

WHAT DOES IT MEAN TO ENGAGE

This next step of the **REST** framework is where it can feel like things get worse before they get better. **To engage means fully experiencing and acknowledging what is happening in your body rather than disconnecting from it.** Trauma often tempts you to shut down or dissociate, but healing occurs when you remain present and allow yourself to feel — without fear or avoidance. This step calls for staying connected with the Felt Sense, the internal awareness of your body's experiences.

Engaging with your emotions and signals invites God into your healing. Rather than letting fear, pain, or discomfort isolate you, you remember that God is present and desires to restore you.

Read the following Scriptures and fill in the blank:

Joel 2:12
"'Yet even now' declares the LORD, 'return to me with all your heart, with fasting, with weeping, and with mourning.'"

Psalm 46:10
"Be still, and know that I am God. I will be exalted among the nations, I will be exalted in the earth!"

What do these verses reveal about engaging with God's presence in the moment?

_____

_____

HOW DO I ENGAGE

Engage your somatic responses by connecting with the Felt Sense and remain present with the physical experience — this takes intentional, purposeful action. Here is how to actively engage with your body and emotions:

 Stay Present — Resist the urge to disconnect, push away, or avoid discomfort. Remind yourself that you are safe and that staying present opens the door for healing.

 Use Grounding Techniques — Help yourself stay connected by engaging your senses. You can do this by placing a hand over your heart, feeling the floor beneath your feet, gently moving or rocking, or practicing slow, deep breathing. A list of grounding techniques is on page 81, and an interactive chart is in Appendix A (pages 114 – 116).

How does your body respond when you remain present instead of pushing discomfort away?

_____

_____

_____

Read the following Scriptures and fill in the blanks:

James 4:8
"Draw near to God, and he will draw near to you. Cleanse your hands, you sinners, and purify your hearts, you double-minded."

When I _____ near to God, He _____ near to me.

1 Peter 5:7-10
"Casting all your anxieties on him, because he cares for you. Be sober-minded; be watchful. Your adversary the devil prowls around like a roaring lion, seeking someone to devour. Resist him, firm in your faith, knowing that the same kinds of suffering are being experienced by your brotherhood throughout the world. And after you have suffered a little while, the God of all grace, who has called you to his eternal glory in Christ, will himself restore, confirm, strengthen, and establish you."

1. I cast all of my _____ on God, because He _____ for me.

2. I can be encouraged in my sufferings because the same kinds of _____ are being

experienced by my brotherhood throughout the world.

3. And after I suffer a little while, the God of all _____ will himself _____, _____,

_____, and _____ me.

THE RESULT OF ENGAGING

As you engage in the present moment with God, you turn from reacting in fear to responding in faith. You begin to experience the peace of His presence rather than the chaos of trauma. Instead of avoiding pain, you find healing in His promises. **By engaging the Felt Sense, you embrace God's presence and promises.**

The more you practice engagement, the more naturally you begin to recognize that God is with you. Over time, you experience His restoration— mentally, emotionally, and physically.

Read the following Scripture:

Isaiah 26:3
"You keep him in perfect peace whose mind is stayed on you, because he trusts in you."

What changes when you stay present with God rather than avoid your emotions?

_____

_____

_____

Exodus 33:14
"And he said, 'My presence will go with you, and I will give you rest.'"

How does God's promise to go with you change how you approach your current struggles?

_____

_____

_____

Psalm 103:2-6
"Bless the Lord, O my soul, and forget not all his benefits, who forgives all your iniquity, who heals all your diseases, who redeems your life from the pit, who crowns you with steadfast love and mercy, who satisfies you with good so that your youth is renewed like the eagle's. The Lord works righteousness and justice for all who are oppressed."

How does recalling God's healing and love help you trust Him with your pain?

_____

_____

_____

PERSONAL APPLICATION

To engage your Felt Sense, explore somatic exercises informed by the work of Peter Levine (1997), Bessel van der Kolk (2014), and Pat Ogden (2006), pioneers in body-based trauma healing practices. Different techniques help at different times — stay attuned to what the Holy Spirit is leading you toward. In your REST journal, reflect on what worked or did not. See Appendix A for an interactive chart (page 114).

Breath-work
1. Diaphragmatic Breathing: Breathe deeply into your belly for 4 counts, hold for 4, exhale for 6.
2. Box Breathing: Inhale for 4 counts, hold for 4, exhale for 4, hold for 4.
3. Sighing Exhales: Take a deep breath and let it out with an audible sigh to release tension.

Body Awareness
4. Progressive Muscle Relaxation: Tense and release each muscle group, starting at your feet and moving upward.
5. Body Scan Meditation: Lie down and mentally scan your body for tension, releasing areas of tightness.
6. Grounding with Your Senses: Name 5 things you see, 4 you feel, 3 you hear, 2 you smell, and 1 you taste.

Movement
7. Somatic Shaking: Gently shake your body (hands, legs, shoulders) to release pent-up tension.
8. Gentle Stretching: Focus on neck rolls, shoulder stretches, and hip openers to ease tightness.
9. Somatic Walking: Walk slowly and notice the sensation of your feet on the ground with each step.
10. Dance Freely: Turn on music and move intuitively to shake off stress.

Touch and Pressure
11. Self-Hug: Wrap your arms around yourself and squeeze gently for comfort and grounding.
12. Butterfly Hug: Cross your arms over your chest and gently tap each shoulder alternately.
13. Foot Massage: Roll your foot over a tennis ball to release tension and ground yourself.

Mind-Body Connection
14. Hand-to-Heart Exercise: Place one hand on your chest and one on your belly, focusing on the warmth and rhythm of your body.
15. Self-Compassion Script: Repeat affirmations like, "I am safe. I am enough. I can handle this."
16. Visualization: Imagine a calming scene (like a beach or forest) and "feel" yourself there.

Nervous System Regulation
17. Vagus Nerve Toning: Hum, sing, or gargle water to stimulate the vagus nerve and calm your system.
18. Cold Exposure: Place a cold cloth on your face or splash cold water to reset your nervous system.
19. Pendulation: Focus on a small area of discomfort, then shift to an area of ease, going back and forth.

Journaling and Expression
20. Somatic Journaling: Write about where in your body you feel stress and what it might need.
21. Expressive Drawing: Use colors and freehand shapes to express emotions trapped in your body.

Tactile and Grounding Tools
22. Weighted Blanket: Use one to calm your body and reduce a racing heart.
23. Squeezing Stress Balls: Relieve tension through your hands by squeezing and releasing.

Journal – Do the following exercises:

- Think of a time when you disengaged from what you were feeling. What happened as a result?
- What is one way you can intentionally practice staying present this week?
- How does knowing that God meets you in pain change your perspective on engaging?
- Write a prayer asking God to help you remain present in your healing journey.

Journal:

_____

_____

_____

_____

_____

_____

_____

_____

_____

_____

_____

_____

_____

_____

_____

_____

_____

_____

_____

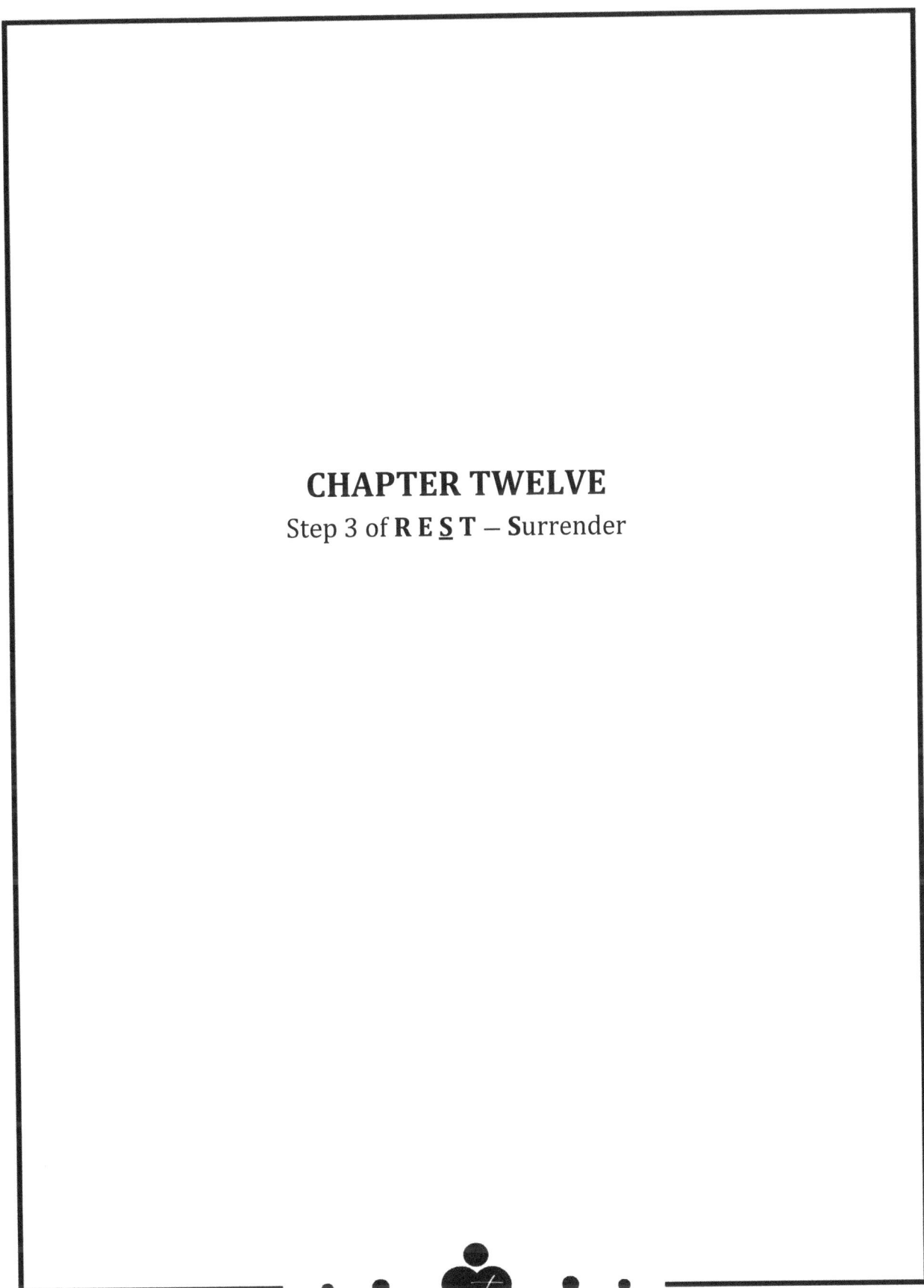

CHAPTER TWELVE

Step 3 of **R E S T** – **Surrender**

STEP 3 OF R<u>E</u>S<u>T</u> – SURRENDER

Action: Surrender
How: Allow the body to process and release without resistance – Express the emotion
Result: Experience God's comfort and peace

THE TRAUMA CYCLE AND ITS IMPACT ON THE BODY

The trauma cycle is the body's repeated response to unresolved distress. When a traumatic event happens, the nervous system activates survival responses — fight, flight, freeze, or fawn (Appendix A, page 113) — to protect you. If this response is not fully processed, the body becomes stuck in a loop, reacting as if the threat is still present — even long after the danger has passed.

Repeating the loop keeps your nervous system in survival mode and can be reactivated even when the original trauma is over. **Triggers** — such as a sound, smell, tone of voice, or relational conflict — can reignite the trauma response. The nervous system may interpret these neutral or mild experiences as dangerous because the original trauma was never resolved or still needs intentional healing.

When the cycle continues unchecked, the mind and body remain in a state of hypervigilance or shutdown — often without your conscious awareness.

This ongoing stress can lead to:
- Chronic tension or fatigue
- Emotional outbursts or numbness
- Avoidance of people, places, or responsibilities
- Difficulty feeling safe
- Physical illness or immune system challenges

If not addressed, trauma lingers — keeping both the mind and body in a constant state of unrest.

WHAT DOES IT MEAN TO SURRENDER

This third step **REST** begins the process of completing the trauma cycle through surrender.

To surrender means allowing the body to process what it has been holding. Instead of resisting or suppressing physical reactions like shaking, crying, or deep sighing, surrender involves acknowledging that these as natural ways the body releases trauma – signs that your body is trying to heal.

Surrender also involves staying present in the moment and welcoming God into that space. His presence is never far. He meets you in the processing, not just after it. As you surrender, you create space for healing — allowing your body to complete what it was once unable to finish.

This is where restoration begins.

Read the following Scripture and fill in the blanks:

Romans 8:26-28

"Likewise the Spirit helps us in our weakness. For we do not know what to pray for as we ought, but the Spirit himself intercedes for us with groanings too deep for words. And he who searches hearts knows what is the mind of the Spirit, because the Spirit intercedes for the saints according to the will of God. And we know that for those who love God all things work together for good, for those who are called according to his purpose."

1. The Spirit helps me in my _____ by interceding for me with groaning too deep for words.

2. For those who love God, all things work together for _____, for those who are called according

to His purpose.

HOW DO I SURRENDER

Much like surrendering the mind in the **SHIFT** framework, surrendering somatic responses is a choice. **Surrender your somatic responses by allowing the body to process without resistance.** Let your body express what it has been holding — without judgment, without forcing, and without shutting it down. Trust that as you stay present in the experience, God's healing presence is at work, and His promises will prevail over the weight, pain, or tension you carry. Here are steps to practice surrender:

1 **Express the Emotion** — Allow the body and emotions to move, release, and flow under God's care.

2 **Invite God's Presence into the Pain** — Imagine His peace surrounding the areas of tension, heaviness, or distress in your body. Picture His light filling those spaces with warmth and comfort.

3 **Be Patient** — Give your body time to complete the cycle. Do not force or rush the process — healing unfolds in time.

What changes did you notice in your body, emotions, or sense of peace as you surrendered? How did you experience God's presence in that moment?

_____

_____

_____

_____

_____

_____

What resistance did you feel — physically, emotionally, or spiritually—when you tried to let go? What helped you release it into God's hands?

_____

_____

_____

_____

Read the following Scriptures and fill in the blanks:

Matthew 11:28-29
"Come to me, all who labor and are heavy laden, and I will give you rest. Take my yoke upon you, and learn from me, for I am gentle and lowly in heart, and you will find rest for your souls."

1. Jesus invites all who are _____ and _____ to come to Him and find rest.

2. When I embrace His call, I am invited into a relationship where He teaches me through His gentle love

and humility, offering _____ for my soul.

2 Corinthians 1:3-4
"Blessed be the God and Father of our Lord Jesus Christ, the Father of mercies and God of all comfort, who comforts us in all our affliction, so that we may be able to comfort those who are in any affliction, with the comfort with which we ourselves are comforted by God."

1. God is the Father of mercies and the God of all _____ who comforts me in all

my _____.

2. The comfort I receive from God enables me to _____ others in my time of _____.

THE RESULT OF SURRENDERING

Recognizing and engaging your body's burdens during a trauma cycle allows you to surrender them to Jesus. **When you surrender your pain, you create room to experience God's comfort and peace.** Surrendering does not necessarily remove your immediate struggles, trauma cycles, or challenging circumstances. Instead, it opens the door for His presence to meet you in those painful and wounded places. Amid trauma cycles, emotional distress, or difficult situations, His peace grounds you and renews your hope, knowing He is at work, bringing everything together for your good (Romans 8:28).

Read the following Scriptures and fill in the blanks:

2 Corinthians 1:3-4
"Blessed be the God and Father of our Lord Jesus Christ, the Father of mercies and God of all comfort, who comforts us in all our affliction, so that we may be able to comfort those who are in any affliction, with the comfort with which we ourselves are comforted by God."

God is the Father of mercies and the God of all _____ who comforts us in all our _____, so that we may be able to comfort those who are in any _____, with the comfort with which we ourselves are comforted by God.

John 14:27
"Peace I leave with you; my peace I give to you. Not as the world gives do I give to you. Let not your hearts be troubled, neither let them be afraid."

Jesus gives me His _____, not as the world gives, and tells me not to let my heart be _____ or _____.

PERSONAL APPLICATION

Below you will find biblical examples of surrendering your somatic responses to God, along with reflection prompts to help guide you in allowing the body to process and express the emotions.

Hannah weeping before the Lord (1 Samuel 1:10–15)
Hannah poured out her soul before God, weeping bitterly, not hiding her anguish. Her body expressed her heart's pain freely before the Lord.

Reflection: When was the last time I allowed myself to weep openly before God? What longing or ache am I holding that I need to release in His presence today?

_____

_____

_____

Jesus in Gethsemane (Luke 22:41–44)
Jesus knelt, fell to the ground, and prayed so intensely that His sweat became like drops of blood, fully surrendering His anguish and fear to the Father.

Reflection: What fear or anguish do I need to lay before God honestly, as Jesus did? Can I give myself permission to kneel, fall, or express physical surrender as part of my prayer?

_____

_____

_____

Job tearing his robe and falling to the ground (Job 1:20–21)

In grief, Job tore his robe, shaved his head, and fell to the ground in worship — a full-body act of surrender in the face of devastating loss.

Reflection: In grief or loss, how do I tend to hold myself back? What would falling before God, fully surrendering my sorrow, look like for me today?

_____

_____

_____

_____

_____

The sinful woman washing Jesus' feet with her tears (Luke 7:37–38)

She wept openly, wiping His feet with her hair, kissing them, and anointing them — a deeply somatic, vulnerable act of surrender and repentance.

Reflection: What act of humility or vulnerability do I need to bring before Jesus today? What do I need to surrender in repentance, trusting that He will meet me with grace?

_____

_____

_____

_____

_____

Next are examples of what this might look like in real life to surrender your somatic responses, along with reflection prompts to help guide you in completing the trauma cycle:

Letting the body shake or tremble without stopping it

Example: You notice your hands trembling or your legs shaking after a stressful moment or trigger. Instead of clenching or forcing the shaking to stop, you let it move through you, trusting that your body is releasing stored tension.

Reflection: How does it feel to allow my body to release tension naturally, without judgment or resistance? How do I invite God's peace into these moments?

_____

_____

_____

Allowing tears to come without apologizing or shutting them down

Example: You feel tears rising when remembering a painful moment. Instead of holding them back, you allow yourself to cry, knowing that God is near to the brokenhearted.

Reflection: How can I surrender my emotions to God, trusting that He is near and will comfort me in my grief?

_____

_____

_____

_____

_____

_____

Taking deep, releasing breaths or sighs

Example: You notice your chest feels tight and your body naturally wants to exhale deeply. Instead of forcing your breath pattern, you allow those sighs to help calm and reset your nervous system.

Reflection: How does it feel to let my body breathe deeply without forcing it? How can I invite God's peace to enter into this physical release?

_____

_____

_____

_____

_____

Lying down or sitting quietly when you feel overwhelmed

Example: Instead of pushing through your overwhelm, you choose to rest, physically laying down or pausing, inviting God into the stillness.

Reflection: What does it look like for me to rest and surrender to God's presence when I feel overwhelmed? How do I trust that He will renew my strength in these quiet moments?

_____

_____

_____

_____

Letting your body express (gently rocking, humming, placing a hand over your heart)

Example: You notice you instinctively want to rock, sway, or place your hand on your heart or stomach. You follow that gentle impulse, using it as a moment to connect with God's comfort.

Reflection: How does God use my body's natural responses to draw me closer to Him? In what ways can I embrace these physical acts as a form of worship and surrender?

_____

_____

_____

Journal – Do the following exercises:

- Journal about the emotions or physical sensations you experienced when you intentionally surrendered a burden to God.
- Spend a few moments today reflecting on any areas you are holding onto control. How can you release those areas to God today?
- Meditate on Matthew 11:28-30 and invite God's peace into the areas of your life where you feel burdened.
- Throughout the day, pay attention to any tension or stress that arises. Pause and take a moment to surrender that feeling to God.

Journal:

_____

_____

_____

_____

_____

_____

_____

_____

_____

_____

CHAPTER THIRTEEN

Step 4 of **R E S <u>T</u>** – Trust

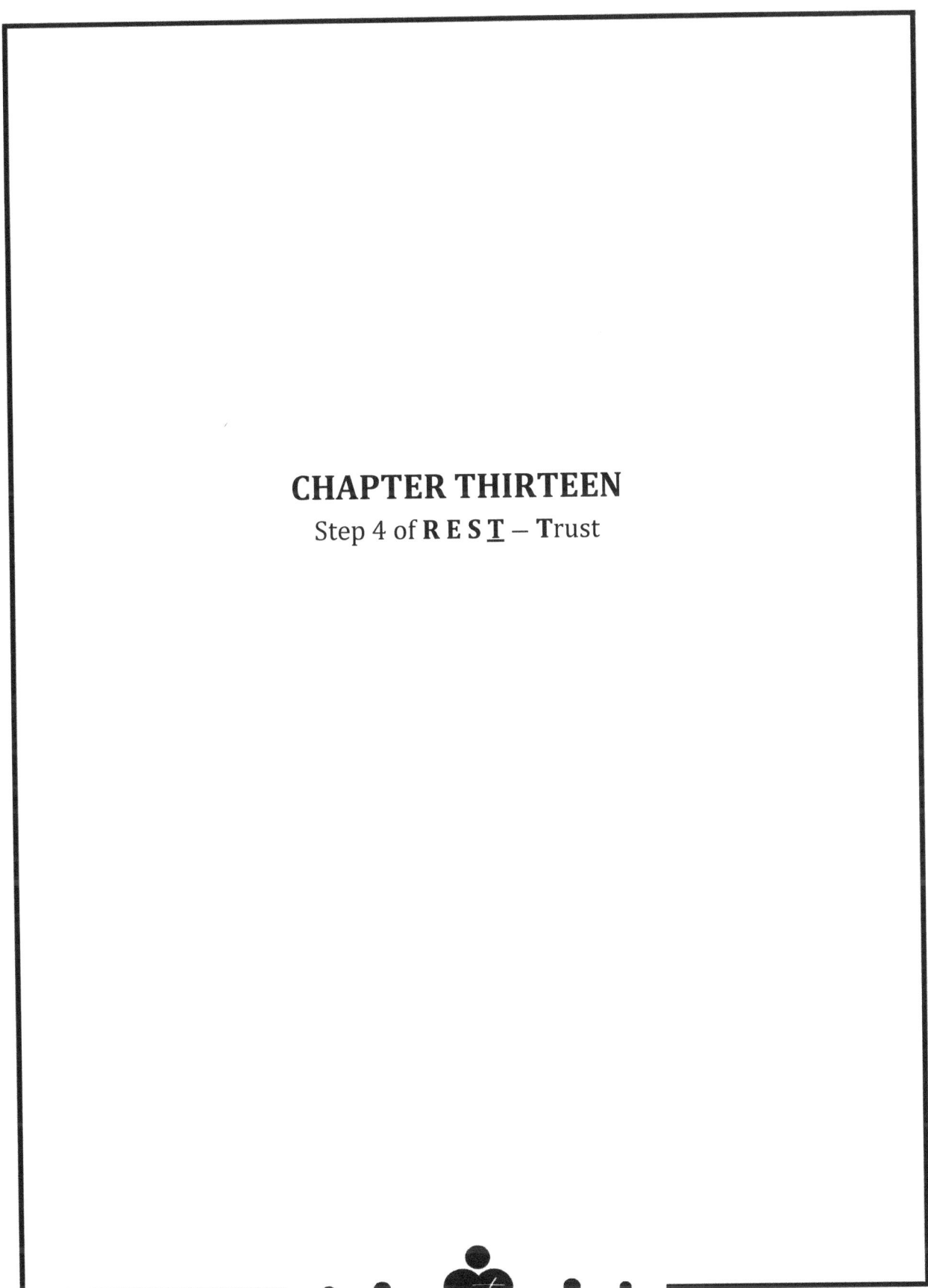

STEP 4 OF RE**ST** – TRUST

Action: Trust
How: Believe in the body's God-designed healing process and trust that the cycle will complete –
Thank and praise God
Result: The nervous system moves from a state of heightened stress to one of safety and freedom

THE END OF THE CYCLE

When you actively practice recognizing, engaging, and surrendering your body's signals, you will eventually reach the end of the trauma cycle. Each person's experience is unique, and each cycle may take different forms, but the transformation that occurs through consistent practice is remarkable. As you continue using the **REST** framework, you will notice how, over time, the cycles become less frequent, less intense, and less overwhelming. While the end of the trauma cycle may not come quickly, with intentional practice, you will begin to notice meaningful progress and experience the healing unfolding in your life.

WHAT DOES IT MEAN TO TRUST

You arrive at the final step of the **REST** framework once you have recognized the cycle, engaged with it, and surrendered it — then, you choose to trust. **To trust means acknowledging that God is in complete control**, even when the circumstances remain difficult or the healing process feels slow. Trust involves letting go of the need for all the answers and allowing God to guide you through your pain. It is about surrendering the desire to fix everything on your own and wholly resting in the assurance that He is working for your good. When you trust God with your healing, you believe His promises, rely on His perfect timing, and rest in His unwavering love.

"Groanings which cannot be uttered are often prayers which cannot be refused."

- Charles Spurgeon

Read the following Scripture and fill in the blanks:

Isaiah 55:9
"For as the heavens are higher than the earth, so are my ways higher than your ways and my thoughts than your thoughts."

1. Trusting God means recognizing that His ways are far _____ than my understanding, allowing me to surrender control to Him.

2. When I trust God, I acknowledge that His plan for me is_____ than my limited perspective can see.

Philippians 1:6

"And I am sure of this, that he who began a good work in you will bring it to completion at the day of Jesus Christ."

1. I can be confident that the good work God has started in me will be brought to _____ by His faithful hands.

2. Even when I face challenges, I can be _____ that God is continuing the process of my healing and growth until its perfect fulfillment.

HOW DO I TRUST

Trust your somatic responses to God by believing in the body's God-designed healing process and trusting that the cycle will complete. Trust is about understanding and accepting that healing is a journey — and it forms the foundation for walking that journey with hope and patience. This step helps transition the nervous system from a place of stress to a state of safety, healing, and freedom.

Below are steps to help you actively trust God as you move through the final stages of the trauma cycle:

1 **Rest in God's Assurance** – Reflect daily on His promises. Trust that He is working in you, even when you cannot see it (Philippians 1:6). Trust that your body is doing exactly what it needs to heal and restore itself, even if the process feels slow. Rest in the assurance that God's timing is perfect, and His ways are higher than ours.

2 **Release Through Prayer** – Prayer is a powerful tool in the process of trusting God. Take time to verbally release your burdens to Him — write down the emotions, fears, or anxieties you are holding onto. Let go of the need to control the process and trust that God is in charge, working on your behalf (1 Peter 5:7).

3 **Shift Your Posture** – As the trauma cycle completes, shift your body in a posture of reverence — open your hands, kneel, or lie down in a posture of surrender and reverence. These movements align your body with your faith, allowing you to fully embody the truth that God is near and actively healing you. **Use this moment to thank Him for what He has already done and praise Him for what He is still doing — even when you cannot see it yet.**

What did you experience when your body's cycle came to completion?

_____

_____

_____

_____

_____

How did trusting God in the process deepen your sense of peace, even if the outcome was not what you expected?_____

_____

_____

_____

THE RESULT OF TRUSTING

"Trust in the Lord with all your heart, and do not lean on your own understanding. In all your ways acknowledge him, and he will make straight your paths. Be not wise in your own eyes; fear the LORD, and turn away from evil. It will be healing to your flesh and refreshment to your bones." – Proverbs 3:5-8

When the amygdala hijacks your nervous system due to trauma or a trigger, and you choose to trust God with your somatic responses, He gives you the strength to endure — even when you do not understand what is happening or why. Believing He has created your body and knows what you need frees you from the desire to control and anchors you in the truth that He is working for your good. **When you trust God your nervous system moves from a state of heightened stress to one of safety and freedom.** In this trust, you move from anxious "What-If" thoughts to steady "Even-If" faith — knowing God is carrying you through. This allows you to exit the trauma cycle and enter into worship, thanking and praising God.

Write out the following Scriptures and underline what stands out to you:

Romans 8:1: _____

_____

John 8:36: _____

_____

2 Corinthians 3:17: _____

_____

Psalm 69:29-30: _____

_____

PERSONAL APPLICATION

Trusting God with your body includes learning to respond to His presence with physical gratitude of the freedom you now have — especially after the trauma cycle completes.

King David is a powerful example of expressing trust somatically.

"And David danced before the LORD with all his might. And David was wearing a linen ephod. So David and all the house of Israel brought up the ark of the LORD with shouting and with the sound of the horn." – 2 Samuel 6:14-15

Reflection: What would it look like to express joy or worship physically without worrying about my appearance? When have I held back my body in worship or gratitude? How might engaging my body in praise help me feel more connected to God's peace?

_____

_____

_____

_____

_____

Try any of the following postures as you move into thanking and praising God at the end of your trauma or trigger cycle. You can have worship music playing in the background or not:

- **Open your hands** — a symbol of letting go and receiving
  - "I stretch out my hands to you; my soul thirsts for you like a parched land." (Psalm 143:6)
- **Kneel down** — a posture of humility and reverence
  - "Oh come, let us worship and bow down; let us kneel before the Lord, our Maker!" (Psalm 95:6)
- **Lift your hands** — to express surrender or celebration
  - "So I will bless you as long as I live; in your name I will lift up my hands." (Psalm 63:4)
- **Lie down and rest** — trusting God's care
  - "In peace I will both lie down and sleep; for you alone, O Lord, make me dwell in safety." (Psalm 4:8)
- **Breathe deeply** — as an act of grounding and gratitude
  - "...and breathed into his nostrils the breath of life, and the man became a living creature." (Genesis 2:7)

As you take on these physical expressions of trust, thank God aloud for what He is doing in your body and soul. He is faithful to complete what He started (Philippians 1:6) — and your trust becomes a form of worship, even when words are not enough.

Journal – Do the following exercises:

- Make a list of what happened when each cycle was completed.
- Reflect on a situation where you have struggled to trust God fully. What thoughts or emotions come up for you?
- Think of one small area where you can trust God more deeply this week.
- Meditate on Proverbs 3:5-8 and ask God to strengthen your trust in His plan for your life.
- When you encounter challenges this week, intentionally remind yourself of God's faithfulness and trust your concerns with Him.

Journal:

_____

_____

_____

_____

_____

_____

_____

_____

_____

_____

_____

_____

_____

_____

_____

_____

CHAPTER FOURTEEN
Applying REST in Daily Life

APPLYING REST IN DAILY LIFE

LOOP OR END THE CYCLE

Trauma cycles have two possible outcomes — they either loop endlessly or they come to an end. When you neglect or suppress the somatic (body) side of healing, you let the cycle continue. This keeps you stuck in a state of ongoing stress, causing your body to store that emotional tension, making it more challenging to heal in the future. The alternative is to break the cycle.

By consistently practicing **REST** during each trauma cycle, you create space for healing. Over time, as you engage with God and allow His peace to transform you, these cycles become less frequent and less intense. By recognizing, engaging with, and surrendering to the body's signals and emotions in a safe environment — and by trusting in God's ultimate design and purpose — we begin to experience freedom from the cycle, moving toward complete healing and peace.

The **REST** framework teaches you how to cultivate somatic awareness — tuning in to your body's signals and using those insights to process and heal from trauma, stress, and emotional burdens. As you learn to rest in God's presence, you can exchange weariness and heavy burdens for His peace and restoration (Matthew 11:28–29). Practice these principles daily, allowing space for God's peace to work in your life and for healing to unfold in His timing.

REST FRAMEWORK

A Biblical Approach to Somatic Transformation for Healing and Resilience

RECOGNIZE

Action: Recognize
How: Identify the body's signals in the moment – Name it
Result: Release the weight of trauma to God
Scripture: Psalm 34:18 – "The Lord is near to the brokenhearted and saves the crushed in spirit."

Matthew 11:28 – "Come to me, all who labor and are heavy laden, and I will give you rest."

Journal: List out experienced body signals

ENGAGE

Action: Engage
How: Connect with the Felt Sense and remain present with the physical experience – Use grounding techniques
Result: Embrace God's presence and promises
Scripture: 1 Peter 5:7-10 – "Casting all your anxieties on him, because he cares for you. Be sober-minded; be watchful. Your adversary the devil prowls around like a roaring lion, seeking someone to devour. Resist him, firm in your faith, knowing that the same kinds of suffering are being experienced by your brotherhood throughout the world. And after you have suffered a little while, the God of all grace, who has called you to his eternal glory in Christ, will himself restore, confirm, strengthen, and establish you."
Journal: Reflect on engagement experiences (what worked/did not work)

SURRENDER

Action: Surrender
How: Allow the body to process without resistance – Express the emotion
Result: Experience God's comfort and peace
Scripture: Romans 8:26-28 – "Likewise the Spirit helps us in our weakness. For we do not know what to pray for as we ought, but the Spirit himself intercedes for us with groanings too deep for words. And he who searches hearts knows what is the mind of the Spirit, because the Spirit intercedes for the saints according to the will of God. And we know that for those who love God all things work together for good, for those who are called according to his purpose."
Journal: List out experienced emotions

TRUST

Action: Trust
How: Believe in the body's God-designed healing process and trust that the cycle will complete – Thank and praise God
Result: The nervous system moves from a state of heightened stress to one of safety and freedom
Scripture: Philippians 1:6 – "And I am sure of this, that he who began a good work in you will bring it to completion at the day of Jesus Christ." Jeremiah 31:25 – "For I will satisfy the weary soul, and every languishing soul I will replenish."
Journal: Reflect on what happens when the cycle completes

MATTHEW 11:28

Come to me, all who labor and are heavy laden, and I will give you rest.

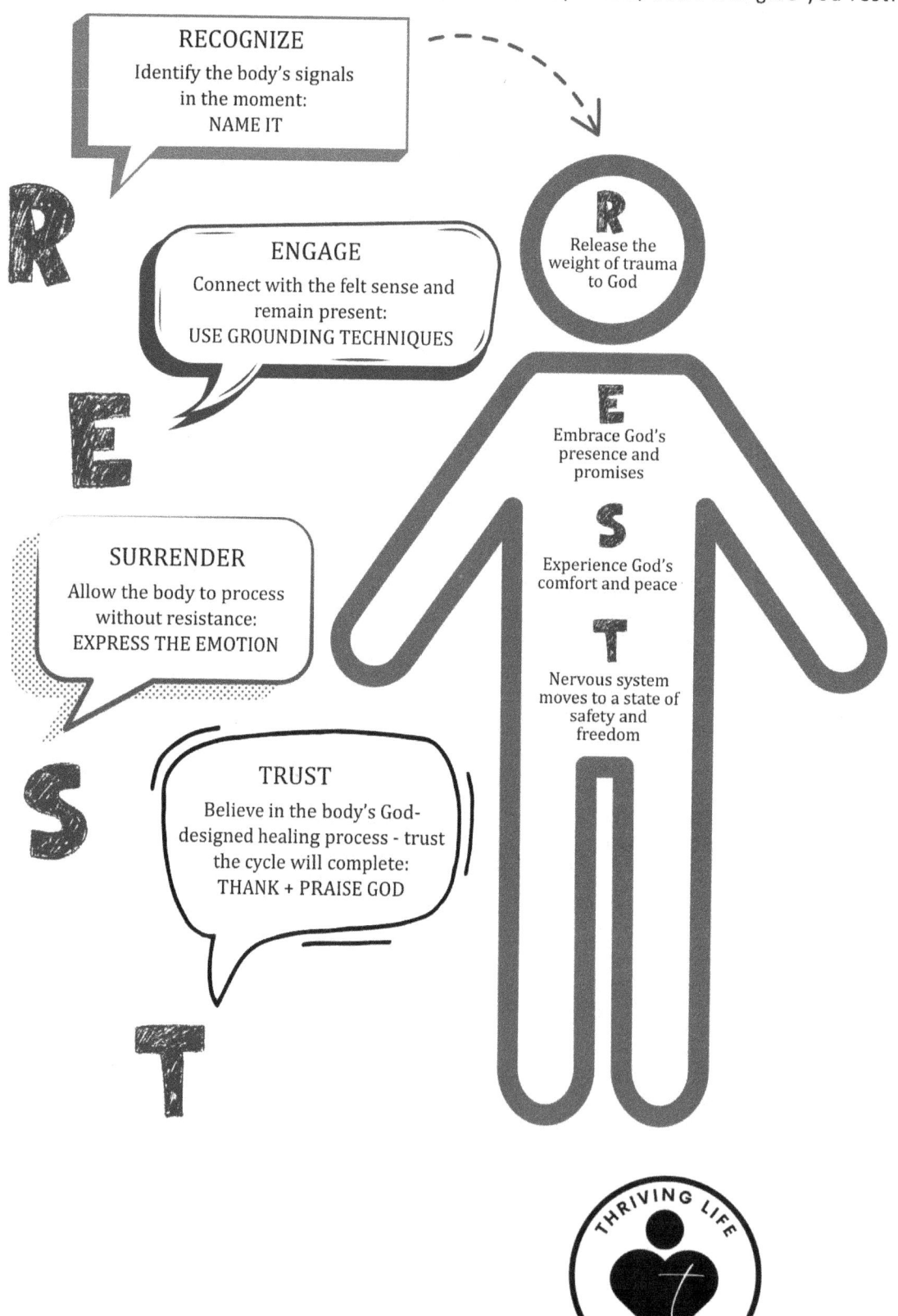

RECOGNIZE
Identify the body's signals in the moment:
NAME IT

ENGAGE
Connect with the felt sense and remain present:
USE GROUNDING TECHNIQUES

SURRENDER
Allow the body to process without resistance:
EXPRESS THE EMOTION

TRUST
Believe in the body's God-designed healing process - trust the cycle will complete:
THANK + PRAISE GOD

R Release the weight of trauma to God

E Embrace God's presence and promises

S Experience God's comfort and peace

T Nervous system moves to a state of safety and freedom

THRIVING LIFE
PHASE ONE

WWW.MINDSETMATTERSCOMMUNICATIONS.COM

CHAPTER FIFTEEN

Making a **SHIFT** in the mindset and
learning how to **REST** in the God's presence

RECAP
Making a SHIFT in the mindset and learning how to REST in God's presence

INTEGRATING SHIFT AND REST FOR LONG-TERM HEALING

To move from surviving to thriving during trauma, you need both a mindset **SHIFT** and a posture of **REST**. Together, these create a sustainable path for lasting healing.

The **SHIFT** framework helps transform your natural reactions, aligning your thoughts with God's truth (Colossians 3:2). It moves you from fear-driven responses to faith-filled trust, opening your heart to God's transforming power.

The **REST** framework cultivates somatic awareness — tuning in to your body's signals — and teaches you to release burdens by resting in God's presence (Matthew 11:28–29). This physical and spiritual rest invites God's peace to penetrate emotional wounds, restoring both body and soul.

COMBINING FRAMEWORKS

SHIFT and **REST** work hand in hand to address both the cognitive and somatic aspects of trauma.

- **SHIFT** recalibrates your mindset, focusing your thoughts on God's promises instead of your pain.
- **REST** anchors your body, helping you release emotional strain and receive God's peace.

Together, they create a holistic healing approach — breaking trauma cycles, fostering resilience, and empowering you to respond with renewed strength and trust.

CONGRATULATIONS

You have now completed this phase of your journey, learning to shift your mindset and bring your body to rest. These frameworks are your practical tools to navigate trauma, deepen your trust in God, and confidently step into ongoing healing. Wherever you began, you have drawn closer to God, discovered resilience within yourself, and laid a foundation of strength and hope for the future.

Now, it is time to assess what you have learned. Take the following two assessments to test your understanding and reinforce the principles that will continue to guide your healing.

Assessment 1

Take this *SHIFT Framework Assessment* to help put these biblical principles to memory:

1. What is the action step for "Surrender" in the **SHIFT** framework?
A) Letting go of fear and trusting your emotions
B) Surrendering to God's plan through prayer
C) Focusing on what is pure and lovely
D) Giving thanks in all circumstances

2. Which Scripture reminds us that faith comes from hearing the Word of Jesus?
A) Romans 10:17
B) Philippians 4:6
C) Jeremiah 29:11
D) 1 John 4:1

3. What does "Invite In" encourage you to cultivate?
A) Gratitude and appreciation for God's blessings
B) Fear and control over circumstances
C) Perfection and self-reliance
D) Analyzing every situation in great detail

4. How do you "Find" peace according to the **SHIFT** framework?
A) By setting your mind on the things above and entrusting your cares to the Lord
B) By fixing every problem before trusting God
C) By waiting until everything makes sense
D) By ignoring emotions and moving forward quickly

5. What is the final step, "Thrive," about?
A) Trusting in God's process and rejoicing in His faithfulness
B) Working harder to prove your worth
C) Seeking approval from others
D) Waiting for perfect conditions before taking action

Answers: 1(B), 2(A), 3(A), 4(A), 5(A)

Journal:

_____

_____

_____

_____

_____

Assessment 2

Take this *REST Framework Assessment* to help put these biblical principles to memory:

1. What is the action step for "Recognize" in the **REST** framework?
A) Connect with the Felt Sense
B) Acknowledge the body's signals and tell God
C) Trust the healing process
D) Focus on what is noble and true

2. Which Scripture reminds us to cast all our anxieties on God because He cares for us?
A) Romans 8:6
B) Psalm 46:1-2
C) Matthew 11:28-30
D) 1 Peter 5:7

3. What results from engaging with the Felt Sense and staying present?
A) Peace
B) Trust
C) Embrace God's presence and promises
D) Self-control

4. What does "Surrender" involve in the **REST** framework?
A) Allowing the body to process and release without resistance
B) Acknowledging God's control through prayer
C) Connecting with the Word to hear God's voice
D) Focusing on gratitude and thanksgiving

5. What results from trusting the body's healing process and God's promises?
A) Self-control & Strength
B) The Nervous System enters a State of Safety and Freedom
C) Thanksgiving & Hope
D) Praise & Purpose

Answers: 1(B), 2(D), 3(C), 4(A), 5(B)

Journal:

_____

_____

_____

_____

_____

PERSONAL ACTION PLAN

As you complete this trauma workbook and step into perseverance, here are some practical steps to help you stay grounded and move forward with resilience.

 Develop a Personalized SHIFT and REST Routine

Consistency is key — true transformation comes through daily practice. Establish a routine that incorporates the **SHIFT** and **REST** frameworks, which will allow you to reframe your mindset and bring your body into a state of peace.

 Identify Scriptures for Ongoing Encouragement.

God's Word is a powerful source of strength and renewal. Find key Scriptures that speak to your healing journey and keep them visible — write them in a journal, post them on your mirror, or save them as reminders on your phone.

 Five Practical Steps for Managing Stress, Overwhelm, and Uncertainty

When challenges arise, these simple actions can help you regain focus and peace:

When you feel stressed – Take a walk.
- Walking helps clear your mind, reduce stress, and restore perspective. It engages your body in movement, allowing you to process emotions and refocus.

When you feel at a loss – Take a nap.
- Rest is essential for clarity and renewal. A short nap can refresh your mind and provide the energy needed to face challenges with a clearer perspective.

When you feel overwhelmed – Breathe deeply.
- Deep breathing calms the nervous system, reduces anxiety, and creates peace. Try inhaling for four counts, holding for four, and exhaling for four.

When you feel disconnected – Engage in worship or prayer.
- Reconnect with God through worship, prayer, or silent reflection. Turning your heart toward Him can reassure you and restore your sense of purpose.

When you feel hopeless – Write down three things you are grateful for.
- Gratitude helps redirect your mind from emptiness to evidence of God's presence.

By integrating these principles into your daily life, you will continue growing and healing and moving toward the peace and purpose God has for you.

Journal:

_____

_____

_____

_____

_____

_____

_____

_____

_____

_____

_____

_____

_____

_____

_____

_____

_____

_____

_____

_____

_____

_____

_____

CHAPTER SIXTEEN
Moving Forward –
The Journey Continues: Healing Workbook

MOVING FORWARD
The Journey Continues: Healing Workbook

MOVING FORWARD

As you close the pages of this first workbook, take a moment to reflect on the incredible journey you have already begun. The **SHIFT** and **REST** frameworks have laid the foundation for a mindset anchored in God's truth and peace. This initial step in overcoming trauma has equipped you with practical tools to process pain, surrender burdens, and trust in God's healing work. But remember — the journey does not end here. True, lasting healing is an ongoing process that involves not only the renewal of the mind but also the deep emotional and spiritual restoration of the body and soul — this is the **subconscious level of healing**, where God continues to work beneath the surface, shaping you into wholeness.

To continue your healing journey, I encourage you to move into the next phase of the **Thriving Life™** method with the next workbook in the series — The **Healing Workbook**. This second phase introduces two powerful frameworks, **FOCUS** and **ACT**, designed to help you assess your progress, align your life with God's purpose, and ensure you are truly healing.

The **FOCUS** framework will guide you in examining your thoughts, emotions, and behaviors, helping you stay centered on God's truth (Colossians 3:2) and move beyond past trauma into the fullness of what He has for you.

The **ACT** framework will empower you to live out the changes you have made, taking intentional steps that reflect the healing and transformation God is working in you. It will help you take responsibility for your progress and continue growing in faith, courage, and purpose.

By engaging with these next tools, you will continue to strengthen your healing and step confidently into your God-given calling. Remember — you are not alone. God is with you every step, restoring, guiding, and empowering you to live in the freedom and peace He has promised.

MINDSET MATTERS IN TRAUMA AND HEALING WORKBOOK SERIES

- **Book 1:** The **Trauma Workbook** has equipped you with the tools to shift your mindset and find physical rest in God's presence as you begin the healing process.

- **Book 2:** The **Healing Workbook** will take you deeper, guiding you through the **FOCUS** and **ACT** frameworks to align your journey with God's purpose and ensure you are truly healing in mind, body, and spirit.

This is just the beginning of your journey toward emotional, spiritual, and physical wholeness. You are now empowered to move from surviving to thriving. With the tools and truth found in The Healing Workbook, you can confidently step into the future God has prepared for you.

APPENDIX A
Charts

CHARTS

Here are a few charts to help you reflect on your experiences as you work through Chapter 1. Use them to label or fill in events, identify types of trauma, and gain clarity on how they have affected you emotionally, physically, and mentally.

TRAUMA PROCESSING CHART

Life-Altering Events	Categories	Types of Trauma
Relational	Conflicts, betrayals, breakups, divorce, loss	Emotional or Psychological Trauma
Physical Health	Severe illness, injury, disability, abuse	Physical Trauma
Mental Health	Depression, anxiety, emotional abuse, breakdowns	Emotional or Psychological Trauma
Financial	Bankruptcy, unemployment, debt, financial loss	Acute Trauma, Chronic Trauma
Career/Professional	Job loss, career transitions, workplace conflict	Acute Trauma, Chronic Trauma
Spiritual/Existential	Crises of faith, loss of purpose, awakenings	Emotional or Psychological Trauma
Social	Bullying, humiliation, exclusion	Emotional or Psychological Trauma, Social Trauma
Environmental/Natural	Natural disasters, earthquakes, hurricanes	Acute Trauma, Somatic Trauma
Cultural/Identity	Discrimination, identity crises, belonging struggles	Cultural/Identity Trauma
Legal	Lawsuits, criminal accusations, imprisonment	Emotional or Psychological Trauma, Legal Trauma

Journal:

_____

_____

_____

_____

_____

_____

_____

_____

_____

_____

_____

_____

_____

_____

_____

_____

_____

_____

_____

_____

_____

_____

_____

_____

_____

SPECIFIC VARIATIONS OF TRAUMA CHART

Type of Trauma	Description	Impact
Emotional/Psychological	Disrupts emotional well-being or safety	Fear, anxiety, avoidance
Physical	Injury from accidents or violence	Physical injuries and emotional distress
Acute	Sudden intense events (e.g., disaster, assault)	Shock, fear
Chronic	Ongoing harmful situations (e.g., neglect)	Long-lasting emotional impacts
Complex	Repeated traumatic events (e.g., abuse, violence)	Emotional instability, relationship struggles
Secondary	Emotional distress from witnessing trauma	Compassion fatigue, emotional distress
Developmental	Childhood trauma disrupting emotional development	Long-term emotional, psychological effects
Historical/Generational	Collective trauma (e.g., oppression, genocide)	Intergenerational emotional impacts
Somatic	Unresolved emotional pain manifesting physically	Chronic pain, tension, physical distress

Journal:

_____

_____

_____

_____

_____

_____

TRAUMA RESPONSE CHART

Response	How You Feel	How You Act	What You Can Do About It
Fight	Angry, threatened, frustrated, powerless	Argue, yell, control others, lash out, defend aggressively	Pause and breathe deeply, ground yourself, channel energy into exercise or assertive (not aggressive) communication.
Flight	Anxious, trapped, overwhelmed, unsafe	Overwork, avoid situations, run away, stay busy constantly	Recognize anxiety, practice calming techniques (breathing, mindfulness), break tasks into smaller steps.
Freeze	Numb, helpless, disconnected, stuck	Withdraw, shut down, procrastinate, struggle to make decisions	Reconnect with your senses (touch, sight, sound), move your body gently, speak kindly to yourself.
Fawn	Fearful, insecure, unworthy, desperate to be accepted	People-please, neglect your needs, say yes when you mean no	Practice setting small boundaries, check in with your needs, affirm your worth apart from others' approval.

Journal:

_____

_____

_____

_____

_____

_____

_____

_____

TOOLS TO ENGAGE THE FELT SENSE CHART

Category	Exercise	Instructions	Reflection (What worked/didn't work?)
Breath-work	Diaphragmatic Breathing	Breathe deeply into your belly for 4 counts, hold for 4, exhale for 6.	
	Box Breathing	Inhale for 4 counts, hold for 4, exhale for 4, hold for 4.	
	Sighing Exhales	Take a deep breath and let it out with an audible sigh to release tension.	
Body Awareness	Progressive Muscle Relaxation	Tense and release each muscle group, starting at your feet and moving upward.	
	Body Scan	Lie down and mentally scan your body for tension, releasing areas of tightness.	
	Grounding with Your Senses	Name 5 things you see, 4 you feel, 3 you hear, 2 you smell, and 1 you taste.	
Movement	Somatic Shaking	Gently shake your body (hands, legs, shoulders) to release pent-up tension.	
	Gentle Stretching	Focus on neck rolls, shoulder stretches, and hip openers to ease tightness.	
	Somatic Walking	Walk slowly and notice the sensation of your feet on the ground with each step.	
	Dance Freely	Turn on music and move intuitively to shake off stress.	
Touch and Pressure	Self-Hug	Wrap your arms around yourself and squeeze gently for comfort and grounding.	
	Butterfly Hug	Cross your arms over your chest and gently tap each shoulder alternately.	
	Foot Massage	Roll your foot over a tennis ball to release tension and ground yourself.	

TOOLS TO ENGAGE THE FELT SENSE CHART - CONTINUED

Category	Exercise	Instructions	Reflection (What worked/didn't work?)
Mind-Body Connection	Hand-to-Heart Exercise	Place one hand on your chest and one on your belly, focusing on the warmth and rhythm of your body.	
	Self-Compassion Script	Repeat affirmations like, "I am safe. I am enough. I can handle this."	
	Visualization	Imagine a calming scene (like a beach or forest) and "feel" yourself there.	
Nervous System Regulation	Vagus Nerve Toning	Hum, sing, or gargle water to stimulate the vagus nerve and calm your system.	
	Cold Exposure	Place a cold cloth on your face or splash cold water to reset your nervous system.	
	Pendulation	Focus on a small area of discomfort, then shift to an area of ease, going back and forth.	
Journaling and Expression	Somatic Journaling	Write about where in your body you feel stress and what it might need.	
	Expressive Drawing	Use colors and freehand shapes to express emotions trapped in your body.	
Tactile and Grounding Tools	Weighted Blanket	Use one to calm your body and reduce a racing heart.	
	Squeezing Stress Balls	Relieve tension through your hands by squeezing and releasing.	

Journal:

_____

_____

_____

Journal:

_____

_____

_____

_____

_____

_____

_____

_____

_____

_____

_____

_____

_____

_____

_____

_____

_____

_____

_____

_____

_____

_____

_____

APPENDIX B

Quick Guide – Four Voices

QUICK GUIDE
Four Voices

 God's Voice

Characteristics:

- Encourages peace, love, and truth (John 14:27)
- Brings clarity and aligns with Scripture (2 Timothy 3:16-17)
- Promotes humility, faith, hope, and forgiveness (James 4:6)
- Leads to conviction, not condemnation (Romans 8:1)
- Guides with patience and wisdom (James 1:5)

Tone:

- Gentle, reassuring, and loving (Isaiah 40:11)
- May be still and quiet (1 Kings 19:12)

Outcome:

- Produces peace, joy, and a desire for righteousness (Philippians 4:7-9)

 The Enemy's Voice (Satan and his demonic influence)

Characteristics:

- Promotes fear, lies, and confusion (John 8:44)
- Encourages doubt in God and fosters shame (Genesis 3:1-5)
- Deceptive, appearing as truth (2 Corinthians 11:14)
- Accuses and condemns (Revelation 12:10)

Tone:

- Aggressive, accusatory, tempting (Matthew 4:1-11)
- Can be subtly manipulative or enticing (Genesis 3:4-5)

Outcome:

- Leads to anxiety, despair, disobedience, and sin (John 10:10)

 Your Voice (The Flesh)

Characteristics:

- Seeks immediate gratification (Galatians 5:19-21)
- Desires comfort and ease over spiritual growth (Romans 8:5-8)
- Leads to selfishness, lust, pride, and rebellion (Romans 7:18)

Tone:

- Urgent, impulsive, and driven by emotions (James 1:14-15)

Outcome:

- Results in temporary pleasure but long-term spiritual dissatisfaction (Galatians 6:8)

Peers (Worldly Influence)

Characteristics:

- May encourage comparison, competition, and materialism (1 John 2:16)
- Promotes cultural or societal norms over God's truth (Romans 12:2)
- Can be both positive or negative, depending on the values they uphold (Proverbs 13:20)

Tone:

- Varies based on individual perspectives but often appeals to social expectations or trends

Outcome:

- Can lead to peer pressure, conformity, or a loss of personal conviction (James 4:4)

Journal:

_____

_____

_____

_____

_____

_____

_____

_____

_____

_____

_____

_____

_____

_____

_____

_____

As you spend time in the Word, reflect on who God is and how He reveals Himself. What does this passage show about His character? How is He speaking? Add a chart like this to your journal to record what the Holy Spirit reveals.

LEARNING GOD'S CHARACTER AND VOICE — REFLECTION CHART

Book of the Bible	Chapter/Verse	What is God like in this passage?	How does God speak or reveal Himself?	How can I respond or apply this today?
Ezekiel	18:30–32	Just, merciful, and patient	Through prophetic word; calling for repentance	Choose obedience daily, knowing God desires my life, not my destruction
John	10:27–30	Personal, protective, powerful	Jesus speaks directly; reveals oneness with the Father	Trust that Jesus knows me, speaks to me, and holds me securely
Romans	8:14–16	Intimate, affirming, fatherly	Through the Holy Spirit confirming our identity	Be led by the Spirit and walk confidently as God's child

APPENDIX C

Going Deeper – Learning the Enemy

GOING DEEPER
Learning the Enemy

THE ENEMY: SATAN AND HIS DEMONS

"Blessed is the man who remains steadfast under trial, for when he has stood the test he will receive the crown of life, which God has promised to those who love him. Let no one say when he is tempted, 'I am being tempted by God,' for God cannot be tempted with evil, and he himself tempts no one. But each person is tempted when he is lured and enticed by his own desire. Then desire when it has conceived gives birth to sin, and sin when it is fully grown brings forth death. Do not be deceived, my beloved brothers. Every good gift and every perfect gift is from above, coming down from the Father of lights, with whom there is no variation or shadow due to change." — James 1:12–17

Jesus has already won the battle through His death on the cross. His sacrifice is greater than anything you face — including what others have done to you. You no longer have to enter battle asking, "What if?" You can stand firm and say, "Even if... my God is with me and fights for me." He will not leave you where you are.

Your enemy is Satan — a fallen angel — and he does not work alone. He has an army of demons working to shake your faith, distract you from God's truth, and derail your purpose. But when you recognize his tactics and stand on God's Word, you can confidently resist him, knowing Jesus has already secured the victory.

Here are some of the enemy's common strategies — and how God's truth exposes his lies:

 Deception

Satan is a master deceiver, twisting the truth to confuse believers and distort their understanding of God, themselves, and the world. He seeks to plant seeds of doubt and lies.

John 8:44: "You are of your father the devil, and your will is to do your father's desires... When he lies, he speaks out of his own character, for he is a liar and the father of lies."

2 Corinthians 11:14: "And no wonder, for even Satan disguises himself as an angel of light."

 Temptation

Satan tempts believers through the desires of the flesh, the desires of the eyes, and the pride of life, urging them to disobey God's commands and seek fulfillment in the world rather than in God.

1 John 2:16: "For all that is in the world — the desires of the flesh and the desires of the eyes and pride of life — is not from the Father but is from the world."

Jesus set a powerful example of resisting temptation. In Matthew 4:1-11, Jesus is led into the wilderness and tempted by Satan. Jesus responds with Scripture, standing firm in His identity and refusing to give in. Jesus models how we, too, can resist temptation — not by our strength, but by knowing and speaking God's Word.

Look up and read the following Scripture and write down what stands out to you:

Matthew 4:1-11: _____

_____

 Accusation

Satan is called the "accuser of the brethren." He brings up past sins, instilling guilt and shame in believers, hoping to make them feel unworthy of God's love and grace.

Revelation 12:10:
"And I heard a loud voice in heaven, saying, 'Now the salvation and the power and the kingdom of our God and the authority of his Christ have come, for the accuser of our brothers has been thrown down, who accuses them day and night before our God.'"

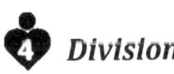 *Division*

Satan causes division within the church, families, and relationships.

Paul addresses divisions within the church, urging unity in Jesus.
1 Corinthians 1:10-13:
"No temptation has overtaken you that is not common to man. God is faithful, and he will not let you be tempted beyond your ability, but with the temptation he will also provide the way of escape, that you may be able to endure it."

James 3:16:
"For where jealousy and selfish ambition exist, there will be disorder and every vile practice."

 Discouragement and Fear

Satan seeks to discourage believers through trials, hardships, and fear, hoping to weaken their faith.

2 Timothy 1:7:
"For God gave us a spirit not of fear but of power and love and self-control."

John 16:33:
"I have said these things to you, that in me you may have peace. In the world you will have tribulation. But take heart; I have overcome the world."

 *Distraction*

Satan uses distractions to keep believers from focusing on God and fulfilling His will.

Luke 10:40-42:
The story of Martha being distracted by serving, while Mary chose to sit at Jesus' feet.

Look up and read the following Scripture and write down what stands out to you:

Luke 10:40-42: _____

_____

TOOLS CHRISTIANS HAVE TO STAND AGAINST THE ENEMY

"But solid food is for the mature, for those who have their powers of discernment trained by constant practice to distinguish good from evil." — Hebrews 5:14

Keep in mind that the enemy is neither omnipresent nor omnipotent. The enemy cannot read your mind, and he must listen when you speak in Jesus' name. Below are helpful tools you are given to resist him:

 The Armor of God

Look up and read the following Scripture and list the parts of the spiritual armor and write a quick description:

Ephesians 6:10–18

1. _____
2. _____
3. _____
4. _____
5. _____
6. _____
7. _____

We are instructed to put on the whole armor of God that we may be able to _____ against the

schemes of the enemy. And to keep _____ with all perseverance.

 *Prayer*

Constant prayer is vital for spiritual warfare.

- **Ephesians 6:18:** "Praying at all times in the Spirit, with all prayer and supplication."
- **1 Thessalonians 5:17:** "Pray without ceasing."
- **Colossians 4:2:** "Continue steadfastly in prayer, being watchful in it with thanksgiving."
- **Romans 12:12:** "Rejoice in hope, be patient in tribulation, be constant in prayer."
- **James 5:13:** "Is anyone among you suffering? Let him pray."
- **Philippians 4:6:** "Do not be anxious about anything, but in everything by prayer and supplication with thanksgiving let your requests be made known to God."

 *The Blood of Jesus*

Jesus' sacrifice gives us victory over Satan.

- **Revelation 12:11:** "And they have conquered him by the blood of the Lamb and by the word of their testimony, for they loved not their lives even unto death."

 *The Word of God*

Scripture is truth and a powerful weapon against lies and temptation.

- **Hebrews 4:12:** "For the word of God is living and active, sharper than any two-edged sword."
- **Matthew 4:4:** "But he answered, 'It is written, 'Man shall not live by bread alone, but by every word that comes from the mouth of God.'"

 *The Holy Spirit*

The Spirit empowers us to resist Satan.

- **Romans 8:9:** "You, however, are not in the flesh but in the Spirit, if in fact the Spirit of God dwells in you."
- **Galatians 5:16:** "But I say, walk by the Spirit, and you will not gratify the desires of the flesh."

 *Faith*

Standing firm in faith shields us from the enemy's attacks.

- **1 Peter 5:8-9:** "Be sober-minded; be watchful. Your adversary the devil prowls around like a roaring lion, seeking someone to devour. Resist him, firm in your faith."
- **Galatians 5:1:** "For freedom in Christ has set us free; stand firm therefore, and do not submit again to a yoke of slavery."

Resisting the Enemy

Submission to God and active resistance leads to victory.

- **James 4:7:** "Submit yourselves therefore to God. Resist the devil, and he will flee from you."
- **Psalm 15:2:** "He who walks blamelessly and does what is right and speaks truth in his heart."

By using these tools and trusting in God, believers can stand firm against the enemy's tactics and overcome in the spiritual battles they face.

QUICK VIEW: TOOLS TO STAND FIRM

Tool	Purpose/Description	Scripture Reference
Armor of God	Spiritual equipment to resist the enemy and stand strong	Ephesians 6:10–18
Prayer	Constant communication with God; strengthens us in battle	Ephesians 6:18; 1 Thessalonians 5:17
Blood of Jesus	Secures our victory over Satan; cleanses us from guilt	Revelation 12:11
Word of God	Sharp and powerful truth; combats lies, reveals God's will	Hebrews 4:12; Matthew 4:4
Holy Spirit	Guides, empowers, comforts, convicts, and intercedes	John 14:26; Romans 8:26
Faith	Shields us from the enemy's attacks and helps us stand firm in truth	1 Peter 5:8–9
Resisting the Enemy	Requires submission to God and active resistance; leads to spiritual victory	James 4:7; Psalm 15:2

Journal:

_____

_____

_____

_____

_____

_____

_____

_____

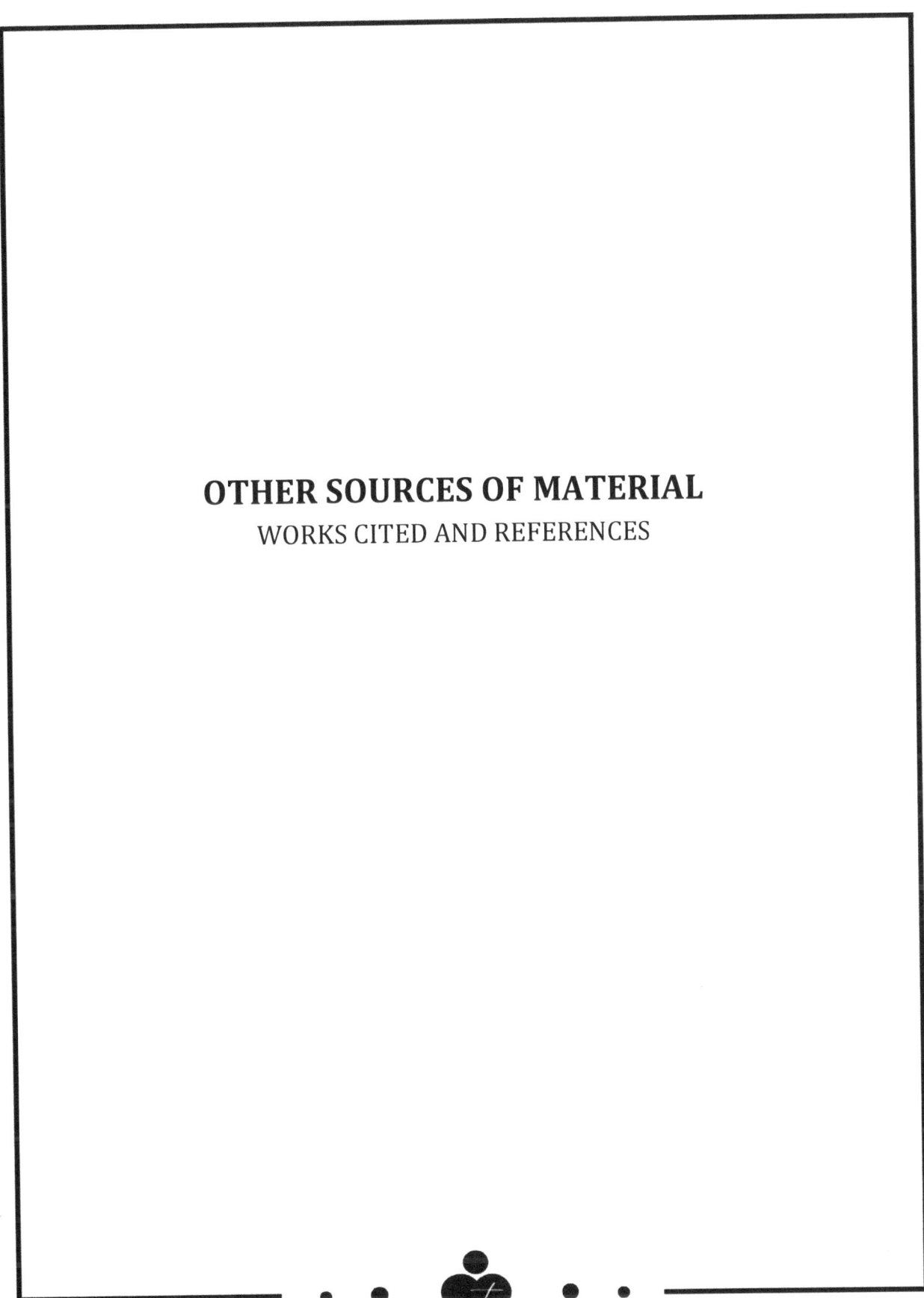

OTHER SOURCES OF MATERIAL

WORKS CITED AND REFERENCES

OTHER SOURCES OF MATERIAL

Works Cited

- van der Kolk, Bessel. *The Body Keeps the Score: Brain, Mind, and Body in the Healing of Trauma.* Penguin Books, 2014.

- Levine, Peter A. *Waking the Tiger: Healing Trauma.* North Atlantic Books, 1997.

- Ogden, Pat, Minton, Kekuni, and Pain, Clare. *Trauma and the Body: A Sensorimotor Approach to Psychotherapy.* W. W. Norton & Company, 2006.

References

- Herman, Judith L. *Trauma and Recovery: The Aftermath of Violence — From Domestic Abuse to Political Terror.* Basic Books, 1992.

- Substance Abuse and Mental Health Services Administration. *Trauma-Informed Care in Behavioral Health Services.* Treatment Improvement Protocol (TIP) Series 57, 2014, https://store.samhsa.gov/product/TIP-57-Trauma-Informed-Care-in-Behavioral-Health-Services/SMA14-4816.

Author's Note on Sources

This workbook was written from a faith-based, biblical perspective on healing, resilience, and personal growth. My research and training were grounded in both Scripture and modern trauma studies, including the secular sources listed above, to help clarify the human experience of trauma.

While these clinical and psychological resources offer valuable insights into how trauma impacts the mind and body, I want to be clear: **true and lasting healing comes only through Jesus**. These resources are included to describe the natural and psychological effects of trauma—not as replacements for biblical truth or God's design for restoration.

I encourage every reader to seek wisdom and discernment (James 1:5) when exploring these materials, and to hold all knowledge up to the truth of God's Word (2 Corinthians 10:5). May this workbook guide you toward both emotional understanding and deep spiritual renewal.